Financial Prosperity

Unveiled

Discover God's _Real_ Perspective

On Riches and Wealth

Financial Prosperity Unveiled

Discover God's *__Real__* Perspective
On Riches and Wealth

Pastor R. D. Weekly

F

Judah First Publishing

Saint Louis, Missouri

Published in the United States of America

by Judah First Publishing, www.judahfirst.org

(a division of Judah First Ministries)

Cover design by Kristy Buchanan, www.kndesign.net

Author photo by Andre Morris, www.dreylamorphotography.com

ISBN: 978-0-6151-9194-2

Library of Congress Control Number: 2008924360

Unless stated otherwise, all Scripture quotations are from the King James Version of the Holy Bible.

For my wonderful wife and partner, who is the picture of a worshiper, and a giver from the heart…

And for my entire world wrapped up in a name—Jesus, without whom I am nothing, can do nothing, and would find satisfaction and fulfillment in absolutely nothing.

Contents

Appendices

Introduction

If ever a taboo existed in the Church, it surrounds practically every issue involving this single word—money. Among the issues related to this all-too-powerful word, the financial prosperity message is the most contentious. As I have delved into the topic, I've found that one cannot simply answer the question—Does God want me to prosper financially?—without considering the biblical and practical implications of both the positive and negative answers.

Ergo, the purpose of this book is quite simply to examine the issue of financial prosperity from a balanced, biblical perspective. I will not only define the term, but will cover the range of issues surrounding it, including both the spiritual and natural reasons why I believe it is such a controversial issue in the Church today.

While this purpose is easily stated, it's not quite so easily accomplished. The subject is not only broad, but also exceedingly touchy. The mere mention of money in the Church often fills people with fear, frustration, and sometimes, downright hostility. So, clearing up the false beliefs that have infected the Church and leaving readers with a clear and conveyable understanding of this issue will by no means be an easy task. Nevertheless, I'm looking forward to our journey because the fruits borne of these truths are wonderful expressions of God's love.

Before continuing, I have an important confession to make. Without apology, I am a "Christian fundamentalist"—whatever that actually means. Shouldn't every Christian maintain faithfulness to the fundamental beliefs and standards of the Christian faith? Despite how secular society may define religious fundamentalism, I consider myself a fundamentalist Christian because I believe that there are absolutes in our faith, and that such absolutes are defined solely by the word of God.

One of the primary fundamentals of the faith is that the word of God (the Christian Bible) is the sovereign and final authority, and that when it speaks concerning *any* issue, it must be accepted as unadulterated, unchallenged, and unrivaled truth. To me, this is not a negotiable position. It is an absolute reality, and applies equally in every situation and to every person. If that qualifies me as a Christian fundamentalist, I gladly accept the label as a badge of honor. I say all of this so you'll know just what to expect as you read this book—a **lot** of Scripture references.

While we're on the subject of expectations, lets deal with

some specific expectations we should have of <u>one another</u>…

Your Expectations of Me:

- Expect me to back up every point I make with related passages of Scripture and applicable explanations (if the context warrants).

- Expect me to label any assumptions or personal opinions as such, thereby differentiating them from biblical fact.

- Expect me to provide thoughtful, well articulated, yet easy-to-understand perspectives on the issues I'll address. This work is intended for the layman to understand and benefit from.

- Expect me to deal with issues head-on. I don't care much for sugarcoating or political correctness. In fact, my direct approach to truth may seem offensive to some, but know that I'm speaking out of love, not cynicism or criticism.

My Expectations of You:

(I hope you will make these your goals in reading this work)

- I expect you to **never** simply take my word for anything. For that matter, don't simply take *anyone's* word as law when it comes to biblical doctrine. Always make the word itself your final authority (2Ti. 3:16-17)—anything less, and you're in grave danger of spiritual manipulation.

- I expect you to read with an open mind, and to be willing to change your beliefs when the word of God has spoken. God's word is so rich, and so fulfilling. Honor it enough to let it determine your way of thinking. Don't reject its truth because it's inconvenient or challenging.

- I expect you to rely on the Holy Spirit to lead and guide you into the truth. Experience, tradition, and personal philosophy are fallible indicators, and should **never** be relied on when searching for biblical truth. If you're unclear on a passage's meaning, ask the Holy Spirit for guidance. Jesus promised that this would be the Holy Spirit's very purpose. (Jn. 16:13)

- I expect you to appreciate God's word enough to consider it more than just interesting reading. Value it enough to put what it says into action. The Scriptures were never intended to simply inform, but to *trans*form. Let them never cease to transform you into the image of God. (2Co. 3:18)

If you take these expectations (both yours and mine) seriously, I have no doubt that we will arrive at God's truth when it's all said and done. And since that's our desired destination, I consider this a journey well worth taking.

The Messenger or the Message

One of the reasons people are so apt to reject the prosperity message is the "prosperity preacher". Unfortunately, people are quick to devalue a message solely on the basis of their personal perceptions of the messenger. For this reason, many believers have rejected the prosperity message altogether.

I must admit that I'm often bothered by the lack of personal, spiritual, and biblical integrity that some who preach the prosperity message walk in. While any honest person would admit that there are **many** prosperity preachers who are men of integrity, the ones who aren't certainly succeed in closing many ears to this wonderful message.

This being the case, I'd like to challenge you before you read any further. Don't be one who considers the messenger before the message. Don't value (or devalue) the prosperity message simply on the basis of who is delivering it. Grow beyond the stage where you reject truth because of the vessel it pours from. Truth is truth, whether coming from a prophet or an ass (Num. 22:21-33).

Value the message! If a drunk off of the street tells you it's wrong to get drunk, don't reject that truth just because it was a drunk who told you. If a man thrice divorced warns you that God hates divorce, don't ignore him just because of his personal history. Truth is truth, period. Now, make sure that what you're getting *is*, indeed, truth. But, once you see that it is (and the word of God should be the sole determinate), choose to accept it.

The message is infinitely more important than the messenger.

Section One

Destroying The Prosperity Taboo

The time has long past for preachers to stop letting heresy hunters (Christians who have nothing better to do than sit around and badmouth other preachers/teachers) keep them from sharing the truth of God's word regarding wealth. I make no apologies for propagating the biblical reality that God wants you neither broke, nor having just enough to get by.

Men like Dr. Creflo Dollar Jr., Dr. Leroy Thompson Sr., Kenneth Copeland, and others have laid the groundwork for the prosperity message. But, it's time for the Church at large to sound God's clarion call altogether, compelling people to understand and walk in the wealth that is their God-given inheritance.

The wealth of the sinner has been laid up for the just (the believer) long enough (Prov. 13:22). It's time for the transaction to finally take place so that the wealth of the sinner makes it to the hands of the just!

So, to hell with the taboos, and to hell with the fear of breaking them. Once you get the revelation that God wants you wealthy, you won't care what the naysayers say anyway. Let's just get the word out and destroy this taboo on riches and wealth.

1

Does God Want Us Wealthy?

L et's get it all out in the open right up front. Nobody wants to be poor. However, more importantly, we need to determine whether or not *God* wants us poor; because if He does, I should end this book before it's even begun.

The only evidence we can reference to adequately deal with this question comes from the word of God. Without it, absolute truth remains hidden, and we're left wallowing in the mire of tradition and personal preference—neither of which is a very appealing proposition.

Having understood our clear and present need for a word from the Lord on the matter, let's determine if financial prosperity is an issue worth examining.

Is it God's will for us to prosper financially?

Not only must this question be answered through the Scriptures (and the Scriptures alone), but the answer is absolutely essential if we're to accurately interpret the rest of God's word on this matter. For instance, if we were to determine that God wants His children wealthy, that absolute truth would (and should) impact the way we understand what other passages have to say on the subject. If, on the other hand, we find that God doesn't *necessarily* want all or any of His children to prosper financially, the effect should be the like.

Let's look at a very good example of what I mean regarding biblical interpretation in light of an absolute truth. The Bible makes a clear and incontrovertible statement that God cannot be tempted to sin (Jas. 1:13). This is an absolute truth. Now, Matthew 4:1 clearly states that Jesus was tempted of the devil, so how does that fact define our perception of Him? The obvious, albeit incorrect conclusion would be that Jesus must not be God. However, that interpretation is blocked by yet another incontrovertible statement the Scriptures make—Jesus *is* God (John 1:1, 14; 1Ti. 3:16). So then, how can these contradictory facts be reconciled?

Apparently, when God was here in the flesh in the Person of Jesus, He did not function or operate as God. This explains how He could be tempted (Heb. 4:15), even though under the veneer of His flesh, He was still God. It also sheds light on a possible reason Jesus repeatedly referred to Himself as the "Son of man" in the gospels.

As you can see, absolute truths definitely affect how we interpret the Scriptures, as well they should. In terms of our present examination, our first goal is to determine in an absolute sense if it is

God's will for us to prosper financially. The answer to this question will influence how we interpret related passages, and will allow us to maintain the harmony of the Scriptures in our interpretations.

"But thou shalt remember the LORD thy God: for it is he that giveth thee power to get wealth, that he may establish his covenant which he swore unto thy fathers, as it is this day."

Deuteronomy 8:18

This passage was directed to the Israelites over 2500 years ago. It states that God empowered them (the Israelites) to get wealth as a result of His covenant with Abraham, Isaac, and Jacob (the patriarchs of the Hebrew nation and faith).

The question is: Why would God empower the Israelites to get wealth if it wasn't His will for them to be wealthy? This would be the equivalent of God empowering Hitler to massacre the Jews, something we certainly know was not His will. To believe that God would supernaturally empower us to an end that is not His will would be neither logical, nor biblical. In fact, it would be contrary to His very nature to do such a thing.

For those who are anti-prosperity (or at the very least, those who don't believe God *necessarily* wants His children to prosper financially), it would be easy to dismiss this promise as only applying to the Israelites. But, you have to remember that we, the Christian Church, have been grafted onto the very same tree of God's people. We are joint heirs of the promise together with the natural children of

11

Israel. In fact, we're now the spiritual children of Israel and have equal rights to this promise. (Ro. 11:17; Gal. 3:29; Eph. 3:6)

If God wanted the Israelites wealthy (and He does), He also wants us wealthy (and He does). If God empowered *them* to get wealth (and He did), He has also empowered *us* to get wealth (and He has)!

But, along with this wonderful revelation comes a horrible implication. If God has empowered us to get wealth, yet we're not wealthy (and not interested in *becoming* wealthy [for His purposes]), it can mean nothing but that we are squandering this supernatural, God-given empowerment (anointing). Not only that, but it also means we are either directly or indirectly choosing to live outside of His perfect will; because apparently, His *will* (according to the Promise) is for us to "get wealth".

Let's examine God's promise to the Israelites (and to us) a little more closely.

> "The LORD shall open unto thee his good treasure, the heaven to give the rain unto thy land in his season, and to bless all the work of thine hand: and thou shalt lend unto many nations, and thou shalt not borrow."
>
> Deuteronomy 28:12

It is abundantly clear that God wants His children wealthy. This passage makes the bold statement that God desires for us to *lend* and not borrow. But, what have we done instead? We have mortgages, car loans, credit cards, lines of credit, student loans... the list goes on and on. No matter how personally acceptable these forms of debt have become in the lives of believers, they are the exact opposite of what God wants for us.

> *"Let the LORD be magnified, which hath pleasure in the*
> *prosperity of his servant."*
>
> *Psalm 35:27*

Oftentimes, we must be very careful how we interpret a particular passage because of its ambiguity. Fortunately, this is not one of those times. In this passage, King David makes a clear and obvious statement—God takes pleasure in the prosperity of His servant. If this is true (and we are constrained to believe it is), we've just discovered a very key principle: God is *pleased* when we prosper.

Some may question the universality of this passage, supposing that David was referring solely to himself as the servant that God took pleasure in prospering. While I agree that David himself was the servant spoken of, we cannot and should not assume that this passage should not be universally applied. The book of Acts 10:34 tells us why this would be a mistake.

> *"Then Peter opened his mouth, and said, Of a truth I*
> *perceive that God is no respecter of persons"*
>
> *Acts 10:34*

God does not honor one individual above another solely on the basis of his/her existence. If God honors one and not another, there *must* be a reason, otherwise God is displaying a trait we usually call partiality or favoritism, something Peter testified was outside of God's character.

If the Lord had pleasure in the prosperity of David, his servant, it takes no great leap of faith to conclude that so long as we are truly His servants (as David was), He takes pleasure in *our* prosperity, as well.

Are you God's servant?

Isn't it good to know that God not only *wants* you to prosper, but that it *pleases* Him when you're prosperous? During moments of worship, I often picture God smiling, being well pleased to receive my worship. The thought of putting a smile on His face gives me great joy and an overwhelming peace. I'm amazed to know that I can put a smile on His face by prospering financially.

Let's examine a passage that brings this point home in a very profound way.

> *"Thou art worthy, O Lord, to receive glory and honor and power: for thou hast created all things, and for thy pleasure they are and were created."*
>
> Revelation 4:11

What a wonderful truth. We were created for God's pleasure. As people who love Him, it should be our priority, our life's purpose to please God in every way. The response of a true lover of God is to immediately seek out every way to please him, since that's why he/she was created.

If you consider the previously quoted 35th Psalm, you'll see that one thing that pleases God is for us, His servants, to prosper. So, in seeking to please Him, one of the things we should be involved in is the godly pursuit of total life prosperity.

Now—and this is important—some will say that to pursue wealth is an ungodly act in itself. But, consider that Deut. 8:18 doesn't say that God *gives* us wealth, but that He gives us the power to *get* wealth. This simply means that the God-given ability to get wealth is resident within those of us who are born again. But, if we don't put that gift to use, it will not produce the intended results.

There's more to be said about this supernatural empowerment to "get wealth", including the importance of maintaining the proper balance when engaging in wealth-producing activities. For now, however, suffice it to say that it's clearly God's will for us to prosper financially. However, we're not going to just happen into the wealthy place. We must pursue it through godly choices based upon His word. We'll revisit the actual pursuit of wealth a little later in the book.

I do want to say be careful. You shouldn't simply be pursuing wealth; rather, you should be pursuing the will of God for your life. In so doing, you *will* be indirectly pursuing wealth because that *is* one component of His will for your life. Just make sure that in the absence or presence of wealth, God remains your source, provider, and ultimate goal.

I certainly don't want it to ever be said that I took a passage out of context, or that I twisted the word of God. So, while we've examined multiple passages—all of which have shown us God's perspective regarding financial prosperity—I want to examine even more to ensure that we're not misinterpreting God's intentions.

> *"The thief cometh not, but for to steal, and to kill, and to destroy: I am come that they might have life, and that they might have it more abundantly."*
>
> *John 10:10*

Jesus made a very key statement here—and this is absolutely phenomenal. He expressed His **purpose** for coming to the earth. Think about that for a moment. Whatever He revealed must have been so important to Him, so important to the heavenly perspective, that it warranted His departure from Heaven and His taking the form of man. (Ph. 2:6-8)

So, what does He say about His divine purpose? Put simply, His reason for coming was to provide us with an enjoyable, fully lived life. While that may sound superficial on the surface, a closer examination explains why such a drastic response from Heaven was warranted.

The Amplified Bible translation records John 10:10 as such:

> *"The thief comes only in order to steal and kill and destroy. I came that they may have and enjoy life, and have it in abundance (to the full, till it overflows)."*

According to the first part of this verse, the thief came to do three things: to steal, kill, and destroy. But—praise God—Jesus came to destroy the works of the thief, the devil.

> *"He that committeth sin is of the devil; for the devil sinneth from the beginning. For this purpose the Son of God was manifested, that he might destroy the works of the devil."*
>
> *1 John 3:8*

Jesus came for the purpose of destroying the works of the devil, which were to steal, kill, and destroy. But, how exactly did Jesus plan to accomplish this feat?

According to John 10:10, His plan was to destroy the works of the devil by giving us a full and enjoyable life. Think about that for a moment... Jesus' chosen method of combating the purposes of the enemy was to give those who believed on His name abundant life. Apparently, He knew something that we're only beginning to understand—that the quality of our lives can be a means through which Satan manipulates us for the purpose of stealing, killing, and destroying us. I believe I'll say that again...

The quality of our lives can be a means through which Satan manipulates us.

Through Jesus' blood, then, He not only bought our eternal redemption from sin and death, but He also bought our right to "have and enjoy life... in abundance (to the full, till it overflows)." I don't know about you, but that sounds pretty good to me.

It is an undeniable truth that God is seriously concerned about the quality of our lives. In the previous paragraphs, I've shown why He takes it so seriously. But, how can we have a full life when the range of our experiences and enjoyments is greatly limited because of financial burdens? How can we have *abundant* life when we are living in the exact opposite—financial lack?

Now, don't try to be "spiritual" and say that you can have and enjoy life while you're broke. Don't put on the all-too-common mask and make it seem as though you're perfectly content to have just enough earthly resources to barely make ends meet. That's not fair to you, and it's not fair to Christ—who came to give you a better life.

While you can and should certainly learn to be content in whatever state you find yourself (Ph. 4:11-12), that does not imply that God wants you to be *satisfied* in whatever state you find yourself, especially when the Scriptures make it clear that God has a better state in mind for you—not just in Heaven, but in the here and now.

So let's take off the masks and admit a few things most "church-folk" have a problem admitting. It's difficult to enjoy life when you have bill collectors calling 5 times-a-day. It's difficult to enjoy life when you're hesitant to visit the doctor because you don't have the co-payment. It's difficult to enjoy life in constant physical pain because you have to choose whether to feed your children or buy your necessary medications. Most important of all, it's difficult to enjoy life knowing that although God is pleased with your prosperity (Ps. 37:25), you're walking in the opposite when it comes to your finances.

God wants you to "have and enjoy life". For those who haven't figured it out yet, this is **good news!** Why Christians would fight against this biblical truth is beyond me. There's a very good reason *Satan* is fighting the prosperity message—we'll examine why in a later chapter—but we Christians should be more willing to accept the good that God desires for us, especially when His word so clearly establishes it.

Let's move forward and examine yet another passage on this issue. You may be wondering, *There's **another** passage?* Yes! The Bible is full of God's good will for us, and it says plenty regarding prosperity in general, as well as financial prosperity in particular. Considering how much the Bible has to say about it, it's sad commentary that the preachers and teachers aren't saying much!

> *"The blessing of the LORD, it **maketh rich** [emphasis mine], and He addeth no sorrow with it."*
>
> *Proverbs 10:22*

> *"Behold that which I have seen: it is good and comely for one to eat and to drink, and to enjoy the good of all his labor that he taketh under the sun all the days of his life, which God giveth him: for it is his portion. [19] Every man also to whom God hath given riches and wealth, and hath given him power to eat thereof, and to take his portion, and to rejoice in his labor; **this is the gift of God.**"*
>
> *Ecclesiastes 5:18-19*

Opponents of the financial prosperity message have important questions to answer here. If God is not concerned about the finances of His children so long as they are not living in debt, why does His *blessing* produce riches? Why are riches and wealth considered a *gift* of God? Why would God choose to demonstrate His goodness by making His children rich if He wasn't moved by the state of their finances?

You may need to read that last paragraph a few times to let the implications of these questions sink in. God chose to demonstrate His goodness toward us by giving us an empowerment to prosper—by giving us an anointing to "get wealth". We need only acknowledge it, accept it, and walk in it.

In fact, the Ecclesiastes passage says that it's a good thing for someone to enjoy the results of his labor "all the days of his life." It sounds to me like God wants us to have and enjoy life, to have it in abundance, to the full, until it overflows. The Bible is clearly one-sided on this issue. Why does the Church, which claims on the surface to seek after the manifestation of God's will in all things, choose to accept *just enough* more readily than wealth?

It's vitally important that we stop valuing the prosperity message by our experiences, opinions, or what we were taught by people who either never searched the matter out for themselves or simply refuse to accept it because they aren't experiencing it personally. God's word needs no validation except the fact that He spoke it, and every word He speaks is right and good. Ergo, if He said it, that should settle it.

Hopefully, you now see how apparent it is that God is pleased with our prosperity. Be warned that the next statement I'm going to make is going to sound pretty cruel, but I'm going to tell the truth and hold nothing back.

NOTE: Throughout the course of this book, I'm going to make certain statements that will seem pretty cut-and-dry. It's my prayer that you appreciate my candor because the sugarcoated gospel has already done the damage of producing a lot of immature Christians who can't handle God's plain and simple truth. Thankfully, my calling is not to perpetuate this "friendly" gospel. All I can do is tell it like it is. On to the statement I warned you about…

Many people read Proverbs 10:22 and Ecclesiastes 5:18-19 (and similar passages) and say that God was not talking about material riches, but spiritual. I call those people false teachers and perpetrators of demonic doctrines (1Ti. 4:1). **Do not follow a person who so obviously twists the Scriptures and refuses to repent.** I'll deal with this in specific detail in Chapter 4.

When we don't read into these passages what we think it *should* be saying, it's very clear what God is talking about. Those who would twist the text to mean anything but the obvious do so to their own destruction (2Pe. 3:16). I challenge you to honor God's word enough to take it at face value. It's not hard to understand if you let it speak past opinion and personal bias (2Co. 11:3). You can't go wrong when you just believe what the Book says!

So, what does it actually *say* here in Proverbs 10 and Ecclesiastes 5? It simply tells us that the Lord's blessing produces, or rather **makes** the blessed person rich, and that to be able to enjoy those riches is the gift of God. Sounds good to me. How about you?

Let's quickly examine the argument that King Solomon (the primary writer of Proverbs) was referring to spiritual rather than financial riches. If this were the case, the second half of Proverbs 10:22 would seem unwarranted. Why would it be necessary to say that spiritual riches don't have sorrow attached? Surely, that would be a forgone conclusion. On the other hand, people both then and now have seen how material riches can actually damage people rather than improve them. The wealthy have problems, same as the poor. In fact, there are particular types of problems that riches produce in people's lives. With that in mind, it becomes very understandable why Solomon emphasized that when *God* makes you financially rich, you won't have the added sorrows that riches gained through worldly means often bring.

As if God's goodness concerning this matter hasn't already been firmly established, we discover yet another truth. Not only does God take pleasure in our prosperity and even empower us to acquire wealth, but He also keeps the sorrows that accompany worldly riches at bay!

It's time for us to rejoice at the goodness of our God. Don't disbelieve it because it seems too good to be true. There is **none** good like God (Matt. 19:17). Is *He* too good to be true, too?

The Character of God

We've examined quite a bit of biblical evidence on this issue.

At this time, I'd like to look at it from a different perspective, taking God's character into consideration. As Christians, we shouldn't just seek to know *about* God. We should actively pursue an intimate understanding of His character and Person. The apostle Paul put it like this:

> *"For this cause I bow my knees unto the Father of our Lord Jesus Christ… [17b] that ye, being rooted and grounded in love, [18] May be able to comprehend with all saints what is the breadth, and length, and depth, and height; [19] And to know the love of Christ, which passeth knowledge, that ye might be filled with all the fullness of God."*
>
> *Ephesians 3:14, 17b-19*

Paul prayed for the Ephesian church that they (along with Christians everywhere) would come to understand the full range of Christ's love. It's from an ever-growing understanding of this love that I make the following point.

It is unreasonable to conclude that God wants us in lack. If you understand the character of God—His personality and good thoughts toward us (Jer. 29:11)—it's absolutely impossible to conclude that He doesn't want us to walk in abundance in every area of our lives, including our finances.

Let me be so bold as to say that if you believe it's not God's will for you to prosper financially, you simply don't know His character. If you're not a Christian, I certainly understand your lack of understanding. If you *are* a Christian, I challenge you to get to know the character of the one you call "Lord".

I'm going to move to some spiritual meat for just a moment. I'm going to share something pretty profound, and it's crucial that you don't gloss over the next two paragraphs until you fully understand their revealed truth.

God is **not** a god of unfathomable love. He *is* unfathomable love (1 Jn. 4:16). Love is not simply an attribute of His character. It is the very substance and definition of His Person. Having said that, you *must* understand that He, being love personified, is incompatible with a nonchalant perception of the financial state of His people. In other words, it's impossible for God to actually *be* love and yet not care about the state of our finances.

Since God *is* love, His desire for us **must** be that we have no lack, that we have sufficiency in **all** things (2 Co. 9:8), and that we live in a financial state called "more than enough" or "overflow". **Anything less would be a condemnation of His very nature, and He would no longer be God because He would no longer be love.**

If you're a parent, you certainly know that it's uncharacteristic for parents to desire anything less than the best for their children. They raise them as best they can, pray for them throughout their adulthood, and never stop hoping the best for them.

What loving parent would want their child to have just enough to get by? On the contrary, parental love compels parents to want the best for their children—nothing less than a long, happy, healthy, and prosperous life. How could your Heavenly Father— someone with an infinitely greater love than we could ever hope to express to our children—want anything less for us?

The Name of God

In Bible days, particularly in Old Testament times, people didn't give their children a particular name simply because it sounded nice. They paid close attention to the meaning of names and they gave their children relevant, and often prophetic names.

Names were exceedingly important to Old Testament Hebrews. They were the first windows into a person's character, and they were not taken lightly.

As with the Hebrew people, God also has a relevant name. In fact, He has a variety of names that reveal various aspects of His nature and character. In the Bible, He revealed a name to someone, and other times, they simply ascribed a name to Him because of an aspect of His character that was revealed through a recent experience. Such was the case when Abraham gave the name YHWH-Yireh (or Jehovah-Jireh) to an altar atop Mount Moriah, after God provided a substitution for the sacrifice of Isaac, Abraham's only son (Gen. 22:1-14). Jehovah-Jireh is translated "The Lord Will See", as in "He will see your need and provide". It was a fitting name. Even today, we often call on Jehovah-Jireh, the Lord who provides so well for His children!

Another example is the name of the Lord, YHWH (Jehovah) Nissi: The Lord My Banner, which simply means that the Lord is our means and guarantor of victory. This was the name Moses gave an altar he dedicated to the Lord as a result of his military victory in Exodus 17:15.

As you can see, God's various names always describe His character and nature. Having understood this name-nature connection, consider Genesis 17:1, in which God revealed Himself to the patriarch Abraham (called Abram at the time) as El Shaddai, which was translated in the King James Version as "Almighty God".

> *"And when Abram was ninety years old and nine, the LORD appeared to Abram, and said unto him, I am the Almighty God [El Shaddai]; walk before me, and be thou perfect."*

The word *shaddai* comes from the Hebrew root *shad*, which refers to a woman's breast, the part of her body that provides nourishment **for** and **to** the baby. With this etymology in mind, El Shaddai can be literally translated: The Breasted One, or God the Breasted. This name indicates a very important aspect of His nature— that He is the source of all substance, the one who supplies all our needs (Ph. 4:19). For this reason, many people translate El Shaddai simply as: God Who Is More Than Enough.

The name, El Shaddai, speaks volumes about God's intentions to prosper us. How could God, whose very name (one of many) means "more than enough", not want His children to actually *have* more than enough? Doesn't it all make perfect sense when we consider this revelation in conjunction with such passages as:

> *"Bring ye all the tithes into the storehouse, that there may be meat in mine house, and prove me now herewith, saith the*

*LORD of hosts, if I will not open you the windows of heaven, and pour you out a blessing, **that there shall not be room enough to receive it** [emphasis mine]."*

Malachi 3:10

*"Give, and it shall be given unto you, good measure, pressed down, and shaken together, **and running over** [emphasis mine], shall men give into your bosom."*

Luke 6:38a

*"Now unto him that is able to do **exceeding abundantly above** [emphasis mine] all that we ask or think, according to the power that worketh in us..."*

Ephesians 3:20

Verdict – Does God Want Us Financially Prosperous?

The evidence is abundant, the verdict crystal clear. While some may not want to admit it, the Scriptures have clearly demonstrated God's will in this matter. He wants His children financially prosperous. He wants us to not only have enough money to handle our own affairs, but to be able to lend to others and not need to borrow—not for a new house, not for a new car, not for a college education, not for anything.

This is the heritage of the saints—to have and not need. Because He is our Good Shepherd, we shall not want (Ps. 23:1). So, rejoice in the Lord and be exceedingly glad. Glory in the goodness of your God, your loving God who wants you to prosper and have more than enough! (3Jn. 1:2)

"For I know the thoughts that I think toward you," saith the LORD, "thoughts of peace, and not of evil, to give you an end worthy of anticipating."

Jeremiah 29:11

2

The Purposes of Wealth

Thus far, we've given considerable effort to determining if it is God's will for us to prosper financially. Hopefully, you've come to agree that it undoubtedly *is* His will. If not, you may want to revisit the plethora of passages examined in the previous chapter.

Having answered the question raised in Chapter 1, one could easily jump to the conclusion that God must be pretty superficial and carnal-minded to want something for His people as "unspiritual" as financial wealth. I believe many people jump to this conclusion from their belief that God is not concerned about the carnal things of the world. But, the reality is that God is neither carnal-minded nor **un**concerned about our finances.

But, how could this be the case? Why would our holy, transcendent God desire something for us that seems so carnal in nature? It's very important that we discover the reason behind this. Failure to examine this early on could lead to an ungodly pursuit and/or misuse of wealth. It could even lead to an overall rejection of the doctrine of financial prosperity altogether, as it has already done to so many people. Therefore, we'd do well to understand the *purposes* of wealth before moving forward in our study.

One thing I've come to believe and teach very adamantly is that God is much more concerned about motivations than about actions. While both definitely matter, right actions for wrong reasons are still wrong actions, and wrong actions for right reasons are nonetheless wrong actions.

As Christians, our responsibility is to do the right things for the right reasons. Nothing less is acceptable. Therefore, clearly understanding the purposes of wealth is paramount to determining whether or not our motives in pursuing it are faithful to God's intentions.

So, what exactly does the Bible reveal about the *reasons* God wants us wealthy?

The Primary Purpose of Wealth

"And God is able to make all grace abound toward you;
that ye, always having all sufficiency in all things, may
abound to every good work"

2 Corinthians 9:8

The apostle Paul tells us in this passage that God desires for us to have **all** sufficiency in **all** things. It's easy to read over this passage and totally miss the fact that financial prosperity is included in the areas of total sufficiency God wants us to walk in.

What's particularly wonderful about this passage, though, is that in addition to expressing God's desire that we have all sufficiency in all things (including our finances), Paul provides us with the *reason* He wants us to prosper. According to this verse, God wants us to "abound to every good work," and He sees our sufficiency in all things as being directly connected to our ability to do this. In other words, **where there is lack, there is a hindrance to our service to God.**

If you need to re-read the last paragraph before going on, do so; just don't let the language make you reject what I said. Where there is lack, there is, indeed, a hindrance to Christian service. You can be useful to God with no eyes, but your usefulness is limited by a lack of sight. You can be useful to God with no tongue, but your usefulness is limited by a lack of speech. And watch this—you can be useful to God broke, in debt, or just barely making it, but your usefulness is limited by your lack of money.

You may be wondering how this can possibly be the case. But, those who have engaged in frontline ministry know that one thing is universally true. Ministry costs money! Owning or renting a facility to hold services costs money. Flying (or even driving) around the country to minister costs money. It's not a cheap endeavor by any estimates.

Even outside of "ministry", what if God wants you to pay

someone's rent for 3 months as an act of love. How can you do that when you yourself are in debt and are barely putting food on the table?

Are you seeing how the lack of money, while *sounding* carnal, definitely has spiritual implications? If our desire is to be fully available and useful to God in all things, we have no choice but to walk in financial prosperity (along with all other areas of sufficiency). We cannot abound in every good work—as God desires—when *any* type of lack limits us.

So then, the primary reason God wants us to prosper financially is so that we can have sufficiency to handle any Kingdom-building activities or obligations that may arise in our service to Him. This revelation sheds an entirely new light on passages like Matt. 6:33.

"But seek ye first the kingdom of God, and his
righteousness; and all these things shall be added unto you."
Matthew 6:33

Christians have an unfortunate tendency to present a front as though it's easy to have Kingdom priorities; but the truth is it can be quite difficult at times, particularly when you have other pressing matters staring you in the face. That's why it's so vital that you get this word on finances in your heart. If it resides anywhere else, it won't be effectual in producing God's intended result. Thankfully, He comforted us with Matt. 6:33, promising that when we have Kingdom priorities, He'll take care of us.

Understanding that financial lack limits our ability to advance the Kingdom, it becomes obvious that God must, of necessity, want us to prosper financially. And not only is prosperity His will for us, but this passage shows that it's also His will that we use our wealth for the purpose of advancing His Kingdom in the earth. It's not simply the first purpose we've covered thus far; it's the *primary* purpose. We are to seek *first* the Kingdom.

Considering the vast implications of wealth—and its nemesis, poverty—I'd certainly be interested in knowing why God considers Kingdom advancement its primary purpose. Sure, we've heard Matthew 6:33 for years, but has anyone ever taken the time to find out *why* we should seek the Kingdom first? And even more basic than that, what exactly does it mean to seek the kingdom of God?

Seek... The Kingdom of God

I can't tell you how often I've heard people try to overly spiritualize the phrase "kingdom of God". They've complicated the fairly simple doctrine of the Kingdom. Let's simplify it once again so that we can understand how exactly God expects us to *seek* it.

The easiest way to understand the kingdom of God is to start by defining the terms involved. The Greek word translated "kingdom" in this passage is *basileia*, and refers to a realm or rulership. If we apply that definition to God, the phrase simply refers to God's realm and rulership.

Instinctively, when we think of God's realm, we immediately think of Heaven. This, although true, would nonetheless be a mistaken application in this case. The book of Matthew uses both the terms "kingdom of God" and "kingdom of Heaven", and they don't appear to be used interchangeably, which indicates that the two phrases are not necessarily referring to the same thing.

The Kingdom of Heaven is the place of God's rule. It is a literal location, albeit one spiritual in existence. But, the Kingdom of God is quite different.

Remember that in Genesis 1:28, God handed dominion of the earth to man. Man subsequently handed that dominion to Satan as a result of sin. Through Christ, we regained dominion, a dominion that will not be fully consummated until the Second Coming.

While God exercises sovereign oversight and indirect providence over all that exists, He does not operate in direct dominion over the earth-realm. That's where the kingdom of God comes in. The kingdom of God is not a place (like the kingdom of Heaven). It is the state of being and doing as God requires—the state of His having rule over a person or thing, and the effects of that rule. Now, I know that's a mouthful, but it's really worth re-reading if you need to.

Jesus tells us pretty clearly that the kingdom of God is not a place, but a state of being and doing.

> *"And when he was demanded of the Pharisees, when the*
> *kingdom of God should come, he answered them and said,*
> *The kingdom of God cometh not with observation: [21]*
> *Neither shall they say, Lo here! or, lo there! for, behold, the*
> *kingdom of God is within you."*
>
> *Luke 17:20-21*

The kingdom of God is the surrender to His rule. Rather than a physical or spiritual location, it's an ideological realm in which God is not God by nature but by the choice of those submitted to Him. Certainly, God *is* God simply by virtue of His Person, but I'm talking about the personal submission to Him that makes Him the ruler *of* a particular individual.

The kingdom of God isn't simply within a *person*, either. It's the reality of God's rule over anything: a household, a marriage, a business, etc. When God is submitted to, and His truths are obeyed, that person or thing becomes a part of the realm of His Kingdom.

So, when Jesus said to seek first the kingdom of God, He wasn't saying "live right so you'll go to Heaven." What He was saying was, "Make the advancement of my rulership your top priority." In pursuing Kingdom-advancement, we are trying to enlarge God's kingdom, not by winning physical territory, but by winning the lives of men (mankind)—and all that concerns them—over to God's dominion.

This is where God says our highest priority should be. As far as finances are concerned, we help advance the Kingdom through the purchase of houses of worship, the funding of ministers' salaries, the funding of evangelism and foreign missions, the financial support of Christian radio and television, and the funding of a wealth of other Kingdom-related activities.

When we make the Kingdom our priority, God promises to take care of all the other things that concern us. Let's take a look at this principle in action.

"But my God shall supply all your need according to his
riches in glory by Christ Jesus."

Philippians 4:19

We do great injustice to this passage when we read it in isolation from its context. People get excited when they hear it quoted, and they remind God of it when they pray. But, the majority of people have no idea how to activate this promise in their lives. According to Matt. 6:33, God will, indeed, supply our needs. But, the passage in Matthew clearly shows us that divine provision is conditional—based on our Kingdom-priorities.

Here in Philippians, the condition isn't revealed in the same verse as the promise, which leads people to believe that this is an open-ended promise. However, if you read the entire chapter, particularly beginning at verse 10, you'll see that this blessing was pronounced over the Philippians as a direct result of the fact that they gave to Paul. They sent money to him and supported him on his journeys, even when nobody else would.

The Philippians had Kingdom-priorities, and as a result, Paul pronounced this blessing over their lives. This makes an important point that's easy to overlook. The only people who can activate the Philippians' blessing are those who have Kingdom-priorities (as Matt. 6:33 clearly showed). When you're Kingdom-oriented—more concerned about the establishment of God's Kingdom than about your own issues—God is well pleased, and blesses you as a result.

Jesus told us over and over again that we should have Kingdom priorities. Consider in the model prayer that before Jesus asked God to give us our daily bread, He said, "Thy Kingdom come. Thy will be done in earth, as it is in Heaven."

In this prayer, Jesus showed us that our priority should be to establish God's Kingdom. Notice that He prayed that God's Kingdom and will would be manifested in the earth as it already is in Heaven. **Heaven is the *place* of God's Kingdom, but submission to His will is the *state* of His Kingdom.** That's what we should be pursuing to advance, with our time, with our talents, with our wealth, and with our very lives.

The Second Purpose of Wealth

So far, we've discovered that God wants us wealthy so that we can enhance our role as partners in Kingdom building. Let's dig deeper and discover another reason God wants us wealthy.

"Let him who steals steal no longer; but rather let him labor, performing with his own hands what is good, in order that he may have something to share with him who has need."

Ephesians 4:28

"But whoso hath this world's good, and seeth his brother have need, and shutteth up his bowels of compassion from him, how dwelleth the love of God in him? [18] My little children, let us not love in word, neither in tongue; but in deed and in truth."

1 John 3:17-18

These passages indicate that another purpose of wealth is the giving of alms (aid to the poor). As Christians, we must recognize that our wealth comes from God, and it's outside of His character to desire that we hoard it or store it up as a treasure (Matt. 6:19). God is concerned about the poor, and He expects those who have wealth to provide aid to them.

As a general principle, when God is seriously concerned about an issue—and in particular, how we respond to it—He usually offers promises to those who do the right thing. It's not that He's trying to buy our obedience. He simply loves to reward those who deal righteously. This certainly applies to the area of almsgiving, as well.

He that hath pity upon the poor lendeth unto the LORD;
and that which he hath given will He pay him again.

Proverbs 19:17

He that hath a bountiful eye shall be blessed; for he giveth of
his bread to the poor.

Proverbs 22:9

"Pure religion and undefiled before God and the Father is
this, To visit the fatherless and widows in their affliction,
and to keep himself unspotted from the world."

James 1:27

I could quote many more passages regarding God's will that we help the poor, but you don't need an exhaustive examination. The point is clear. God desires for us to give alms. Why? –Put simply, it's His character to be concerned about those who cannot help themselves. If that's where *His* heart is on the issue, that's where ours should be, too.

In Luke 10:30-37, the story of the Good Samaritan is recounted. In the narrative, a man was robbed while traveling and was left lying wounded along the side of the road. As people passed by, they crossed to the other side of the road and kept on about their business. Eventually, a man (a Samaritan) passed by, saw the man, cleaned him up, took him to an inn, and took care of him. The next day, as he was about to leave, the man paid the innkeeper and told him to take care of the wounded man as he continued to recover. He promised the innkeeper that he'd repay any charges when he returned. That's the gist of the story.

Something that's easy to overlook about this story is that as good a heart as the Samaritan man had, he would have been greatly limited as to what he could do for the ailing man had he himself been poor. How could he have provided medical dressings, oil and wine for cleaning the wound, and a horse to carry the man to the inn? How could he have paid the innkeeper for an extended stay, and even promised to pay any additional charges upon his return? Apparently, the Samaritan's wealth empowered him to follow his heart and help the wounded man, an act that was well-pleasing to God.

As Christians, it should give us pleasure to help people in need. But, when we don't have any money ourselves, it becomes a burden or a disappointment if we can't help. Wealth provides us with the excess that we can use to help others. Poverty, on the other hand, greatly limits what we can do and how well we can do it.

Why should we help the poor?

So often, we stop our search after discovering God's will. But, sometimes it helps to understand *why* a particular thing or action is His will, so that as we fulfill it, we do it in the right spirit. While a full understanding is not a requisite for obedience, and is not always available in a given situation, we should try to get an understanding to ensure that we're doing the right thing the right way and for the right reason.

Almsgiving is important because it is an outgrowth of God's love. When we have genuine care for others, it is difficult not to be moved into action when we see them suffer. Benevolence also has an evangelistic value. By *demonstrating* God's love, we gently lead those we help closer to the cross, and that's infinitely more important than anything else.

The Bible says in Romans 5:8 that God demonstrated ("commendeth" in the King James Version) His love for us in that while we were still sinners, Christ died for us. I can't tell you how thankful I am that God doesn't just tell us how much He loves us, but that He *demonstrates* His love. As we strive to be like God, our love compels us to demonstrate acts of charity, rather than simply wishing the best for people. Riches aid us to this end.

The Final Purpose of Wealth

We've covered two important purposes of wealth. While I've ordered these in a way that indicates the priorities these purposes should have in your life, I don't want to imply that this third and final purpose of wealth is unimportant. It's simply the third of three.

> *"Charge them that are rich in this world, that they be not highminded; nor trust in uncertain riches, but in the living God, who giveth us richly all things to enjoy"*
>
> *1 Timothy 6:17*

According to this passage, God *richly* gives us all things to enjoy. If we can agree that money is a *thing*, we can agree that God desires for us to have it richly—not just enough to take care of our bills, and not just a little extra. God is a God of abundance and excess, and wealth is His gift to us.

Not only does this passage show that wealth comes from God, but it also shows *why* it comes from Him. He gives us *"richly* all things **to enjoy.**" What would appear a sacrilegious statement comes directly from the Bible. God gives us wealth so that we may enjoy it, and we should make no apologies for walking in the fulfillment of this, His third purpose for wealth.

It's sad that so many Christians are afraid to enjoy material wealth because of their fear of being perceived as high-minded or greedy. But, the truth is that God wants us to enjoy the wealth that He's promised us (which we can't do until we actually *get* it). It's a good thing to go to a nice restaurant from time to time, where you order what you want with no regard for the price of the meal. It's a good thing to buy a house simply because it's the one you want; not because it's the one you can *afford*. We have to remember that God takes pleasure in our prosperity.

> *"A man to whom God hath given riches, wealth, and honor,*
> *so that he wanteth nothing for his soul of all that he desireth,*
> *yet God giveth him not power to eat thereof, but a stranger*
> *eateth it: this is vanity, and it is an evil disease."*
>
> *Ecclesiastes 6:2*

We learned in the book of First Timothy that riches come from God. Now, if we connect that reality to this passage in Ecclesiastes, we can have but one inescapable conclusion. It's a great evil for God to bless us with wealth and for us not to be able to enjoy it.

Our enemy has tricked us into perceiving wealthy Christians as less spiritual simply because they're wealthy, or as though they had done something wrong. We used Jesus' warning about the difficulty of a rich man entering into the Kingdom of God as justification for denying riches outright.

> "What fools we mortals be."
>
> Puck, A Midsummer Night's Dream

It's imperative that we shed our inhibitions. When God leads you to the wealthy place, you must **not** let people make you feel guilty about it. Wealth is a gift from God, and there's absolutely nothing wrong with enjoying it. To not enjoy it is actually quite an evil, as Ecclesiastes expressly showed us.

Does God approve of excess?

This is a very important question. If we're talking about financial prosperity and wealth, we have to discuss the extremes of the issue. How much is too much? Can we even have too much? Is there a certain level where we should stop expecting and/or pursuing increase? These are all important questions that every Christian should seek an answer to if they don't want to fall into the traps associated with financial prosperity.

First of all, we'll answer the general question of whether God approves of excess. What I mean by the term "excess" is the state of having much more than you need and/or more than you can reasonably put to use. A good example of excess would be owning four houses (one for each season), seven cars (one for each day of the week), dozens of suits, dozens of pairs of shoes, and more money in the bank than a small country.

I have no doubt that as you read that description of excess you thought to yourself, *I can see how someone could think that's just too much.* Whether you agree with Christians having excess or not, it's understandable where people are coming from. In most circumstances, we've been raised to fear excess, particularly because so many people in the world are without. But, even in light of all these reasons to fear or shun excess, I'd much rather know God's view of it. In the end, His opinion is the only one that matters.

"Now unto him that is able to do exceeding abundantly
above all that we ask or think, according to the power that
worketh in us"

Ephesians 3:20

This is actually my favorite passage in the Bible. It speaks to me of the necessity of faith in every area of life because God can't do above and beyond *nothing*. We must have a request and an expectation in order for Him to exceed it. That's great motivation for simply believing God.

Let's dissect the promise here. According to this verse, God won't dare do just **all** you ask or think. He won't stop at doing **above all** you ask or think. He won't even dare do **abundantly above all** you ask or think. No… According to the power that works within us (our faith), God will do **exceeding** abundantly **above ALL** we ask or think. If there were ever a passage regarding excess and God's desire to give it to us, this is certainly it! Just as a side note, the words "exceed" and "excess" are related words, so this passage definitely speaks of excess.

"And Jesus answered and said, Verily I say unto you,
There is no man that hath left house, or brethren, or sisters,
or father, or mother, or wife, or children, or lands, for my
sake, and the gospel's, [30] But he shall receive a
hundredfold now in this time, houses, and brethren, and
sisters, and mothers, and children, and lands, with

persecutions; and in the world to come eternal life."

Mark 10:29-30

"Neither was there any among them that lacked: for as many as were possessors of lands or houses sold them, and brought the prices of the things that were sold"

Acts 4:34

In the passage in Mark, Jesus Himself makes the promise that if we would just have Kingdom priorities, even to the neglect of what matters most in our lives, we would receive **in *this* life** a hundredfold. But, look at what we'll receive: plural house**s** and plural land**s**.

Now, someone might read this passage and think, *Jesus wasn't saying that one person alone would have houses and lands, but that those who sacrificed would collectively have houses and lands.* But, if we take a look at the first part of the 30th verse, it clearly says that "he" (one individual person) would receive these things (multiple houses and multiple lands).

Apparently, God's promise to people with Kingdom priorities includes an excess of wealth and possessions: multiple houses, multiple lands, and even a large family (although the large family probably refers to the Christian family that the individual would become a part of).

Think of the excess many prosperity preachers live in. If they own multiple multi-million dollar houses, people think they're wasteful, greedy thieves who take advantage of the people of God for selfish gain. But, when you look at what God has to say on the subject, there is simply no way to biblically refute excessive wealth.

Now, take a look at the passage in Acts. The people sold all their excess and brought it to the fledgling Church so that no one would have lack. If these people had been poor, how could they have generated the money to offer this wealth-sharing system? As I've said previously, in the absence of wealth, our ability to offer certain types of assistance is limited.

As I did with the previous passage, I want to quickly address what I perceive are many people's anti-prosperity thoughts about this passage in Acts. Some may think, *Well, this verse proves God doesn't want us to have excess because these people sold their excess and gave it to the poor.*

My response to this argument is to simply warn people not to read into the verse what isn't there. First of all, nowhere in this text is it expressed or even implied that these people were commanded to sell what they had and bring it to the apostles. They chose to do what they did. It was not an indication that God was displeased with their abundance. Quite to the contrary, *because* they had abundance, they were able to help others.

People are often quick to reference the misdeed of Ananias and Sapphira in the next chapter of Acts. But again, people would do well not to read into the text what isn't there. This husband and wife were not struck dead by God because they kept some of the profit for themselves. Remember, they were never commanded to give in the first place.

The text specifically tells us why Ananias and Sapphira were killed…

"But Peter said, Ananias, why hath Satan filled thine heart to lie to the Holy Ghost, and to keep back part of the price of the land? [4] While it remained, was it not thine own? and after it was sold, was it not in thine own power? why hast thou conceived this thing in thine heart? thou hast not lied unto men, but unto God. [5] And Ananias hearing these words fell down, and gave up the ghost: and great fear came on all them that heard these things."

Acts 5:3-5

Peter told Ananias his sin before Ananias died. In verse 4, he specifically said that the land was in Ananias' own power to do with as he pleased (which indicates that God never commanded these believers to sell their property). After selling the land, Ananias could have done whatever he wanted with the money. His sin was that he presented the money to the apostles *as though* it was the entire price of the land sold. In keeping part of the profit for himself, yet presenting the gift as though it were the full amount, he was, in effect, lying to the Holy Spirit. *That* was his sin, and the sin of his wife (vs. 7-10).

Notice that when it came to Ananias' wife, the Holy Spirit didn't simply kill her immediately when the partial gift was first offered by her husband. Clearly, this was because the amount of the gift wasn't the sin. The sin was that after Peter asked if they sold the land for a particular amount, she lied. She was killed for the very same reason her husband was—for lying to the Holy Spirit.

Had this couple just given an offering in an amount of their choosing, they would have been fine. But, they came forward as though they were participating in what was a voluntary, yet specific act of giving.

The obvious question is: Why would they do such a thing? Why would they lie to God like that? Sadly, they were victims of something that so many Christians today fall victim to—pride. They wanted to look good in the eyes of others.

We may snicker at their motives, but how many times do we find people doing the very same thing today—not giving because it's in their hearts to give, but because they want people to *see* them giving. This prideful exaltation of self is hateful to God, for He loves those who give because they *want* to give. He loves the *cheerful* giver. (2Co. 9:7)

Back to the matter of financial excess…

The Christians in Acts couldn't have given as they did unless they were wealthy. Wealth provided them with a means to be a blessing to others. That is, in fact, what God promised to Abraham— that He would bless others by blessing *him*. In other words, Abraham would be a conduit through which God would bless the people of the world (Gen. 12:2-3; 22:17). But, Abraham couldn't be that conduit until he himself was blessed. In order to bless others *through* him, God had to give blessings *to* him. Can God bless others by blessing you?

"Thou preparest a table before me in the presence of mine
enemies: thou anointest my head with oil; my cup
runneth over."

Psalm 23:5

*"Bring ye all the tithes into the storehouse, that there may be meat in mine house, and prove me now herewith, saith the LORD of hosts, if I will not open you the windows of heaven, and pour you out a blessing, that **there shall not be room enough to receive it**."*

Malachi 3:10

*"A good man **leaveth an inheritance to [even] his children's children**: and the wealth of the sinner is laid up for the just."*

Proverbs 13:22

[All Emphases Mine]

The first passage is very familiar. Many of us memorized the 23rd Psalm as young children in Sunday school. But, the power of the passage isn't simply in the fact that the words are there. We've memorized these words, yet have we gotten a revelation of their meaning?

This passage demonstrates God's promise of excess. David said that his cup continued to run over, meaning that he had more than he could contain, and continued to receive more and more—exactly as we see promised to the faithful tither in the second quotation.

How do we respond to such a promise as found in Malachi 3:10? Do we tell God, "No, thanks. I don't need that much," or do we simply accept that He's the God of increase and enjoy His generosity towards us?

As long as your faith can believe for it, your obedience can permit it, and your integrity can maintain it, the promise is that there's no limit to how much God wants to (and will) bless you with. That's very powerful, so I think I'll say that again.

If your faith can believe for it, your obedience can permit it, and your integrity can maintain it, there's no limit to how much God will bless you with! Hallelujah!

In the final passage quoted above, a very wonderful statement is made. A "good man" is one who leaves an inheritance to not only his children, but even to his grandchildren. Today, you rarely find people who even have enough to leave an inheritance to just their first line, let alone their grandchildren. In fact, many Christians are leaving nothing but debt as an inheritance. Surely, that's not God's best for us. (Psalm 50:10)

Well, I think the verdict is in. God doesn't have a problem with excess. Quite to the contrary, He **promises** it to those who have Kingdom priorities. I don't know about you, but I plan on walking in the fulfillment of that promise every day—houses and lands, large families, an enjoyable life, money to sow, money to spend, money to leave as an inheritance... This is the heritage of the saints!

Embrace God's promise despite what others may think. Only God's opinion matters, and we've already seen that He takes pleasure in the *excessive* wealth of His faithful servants.

So again, wealth has three main purposes: Kingdom advancement, the giving of alms, and personal enjoyment. All three of these are God-ordained purposes, and we shouldn't neglect any of them. Once we shed our traditional views of wealth as being a bad thing, we'll realize that the impact that we can have is exponentially increased when we have resources with which to magnify that impact. Surely, this is God's will.

It's time for the Body of Christ to walk in wealth. It's time for us to purchase houses of worship instead of renting, leasing, or financing them. It's time for us to pay fitting salaries for the enormous responsibility we entrust to those who labor in the word of God on our behalf. It's time for us to have houses and lands that nobody owns but us, with no mortgage, and no liens. It's time for people to see how we dress, how we live, and how freely we give, and know that our God takes good care of us.

"He that is despised, and hath a servant,
is better than he that honoreth himself,
and lacketh bread."

Proverbs 12:9

3

Wealthy People of God
In The Bible

If financial prosperity were not God's will for us, we would have a huge logical problem to solve. In case after case, prosperity was a result of obedience and faithfulness to God, while poverty was a result of disobedience. Logically speaking, God would have a hard time promoting financial poverty (or even "just enough", for that matter) as a virtue in light of established precedent.

If, on the other hand, we're to believe that financial prosperity is God's good purpose toward us, it shouldn't be difficult to find examples of prosperous people in the Bible. After all, God is no respecter of persons. We should expect that His faithful servants walked in the manifestation of what we're only beginning to resurrect in Church doctrine today.

Abraham

When talking about financially prosperous people in the Bible, it would only be right to start with the great patriarch of the faith, Abraham. All believers agree that he was a man of astounding faith, particularly when you consider his willingness to sacrifice his long-awaited son, Isaac. What many people don't readily acknowledge, however, is that Abraham wasn't just rich in faith, but in material wealth as well.

> *"Then Abram took Sarai his wife and Lot his brother's son, and all their possessions that they had gathered, and the people whom they had acquired in Haran, and they departed to go to the land of Canaan. So they came to the land of Canaan."*
>
> *Genesis 12:5 (NKJV)*

This passage comes immediately after God makes one of His famous promises to Abraham, called Abram at the time (verses 1-3). In response to God's instructions, Abram set out for Canaan with his family. But, notice that Abram journeyed with "all [his] possessions" and the people they had *acquired* in Haran.

According to this verse, not only did Abram have what appears from the language to be *many* possessions, but he also owned slaves, a convenience afforded only to people with financial resources. But, all that Abram already possessed barely scratched the surface of what God was about to do in His life.

"And when Abram heard that his brother was taken captive, he armed his trained servants, born in his own house, three hundred and eighteen, and pursued them unto Dan. [15] And he divided himself against them, he and his servants, by night, and smote them, and pursued them unto Hobah, which is on the left hand of Damascus. [16] And he brought back all the goods, and also brought again his brother Lot, and his goods, and the women also, and the people... [21] And the king of Sodom said unto Abram, Give me the persons, and take the goods to thyself. And Abram said to the king of Sodom, I have lifted up mine hand unto the LORD, the most high God, the possessor of heaven and earth, That I will not take from a thread even to a shoelatchet, and that I will not take any thing that is thine, lest thou shouldest say, I have made Abram rich: Save only that which the young men have eaten, and the portion of the men which went with me, Aner, Eshcol, and Mamre; let them take their portion."

Genesis 14: 14-16, 21-24

Before showing how this passage is relevant to the discussion at hand, let me give you a bit of background.

Reading from the beginning of the chapter, you'll see that an alliance of subordinate kings rebelled against a high king (a king of kings) named Chedorlaomer, the kind of Elam. Well, Chedorlaomer didn't sit idly by while these kings rebelled. He launched an invasion and quelled the rebellion, taking all the goods of Sodom and Gomorrah (two of the kingdoms which rebelled) as the spoils of war.

55

Included in their spoils was Abram's nephew, Lot, who was living in Sodom at the time.

This is where verse 14 (in the quotation above) picks up the story. When Abram heard that his kinsman, Lot, had been captured, he put together a war-trained band of 318 servants (who already belonged to him) to go and free Lot. Now, of note are two things in particular. First, consider the size of Abram's force. He had 318 *war-trained* servants, meaning that the total number of servants belonging to him (including those who weren't war-trained) greatly exceeded this number. Secondly, these servants were born in his house, meaning that even their parents were Abram's servants. This indicates that Abram's wealth wasn't a momentary excess, but his perpetual state. He was a **very** wealthy man—a patriarch, indeed.

Notice also in verses 14-16 that Abram and his war-trained servants pursued the very same force that defeated an alliance of five kings. Not only did they pursue them, but they drove them out of the land and reclaimed the captured people and goods. Abram's force accomplished what an alliance of five kings couldn't!

Now, the story doesn't end there. When Abram returned from his campaign, he gave a tithe of the spoils to the priest of God, Melchizedek—who was the king of Salem (verses 18-20, not quoted above).

You may wonder how Abram could tithe these spoils when they belonged to the king of Sodom. Well, in warfare, the spoils don't belong to the titleholder, but to whoever captured them. At one point, these goods (and people) belonged to the king of Sodom. But, when they lost their rebellion and high king Chedorlaomer captured these things, they no longer belonged to the king of Sodom. The very same principle applied when Abram pursued this force and re-took the goods.

So, all the spoils now rightly belonged to Abram. He tithed 10% of the spoils to the man of God—and yes, he tithed hundreds of years before the Law was ever instituted. But, notice what Abram did with the remaining 90% of what was now *his* property (both goods and people). In verse 21, the king of Sodom asked for the return of the people. Abram's response was absolutely awesome. He gave a rightful portion to those who allied with him, and returned everything remaining to the king of Sodom. Why? –Because Abram didn't want any man to think his possessions made Abraham wealthy. Abram recognized something we'd do well to understand today…

God, not man, is our source.

Just for a minute, let's take off the "religious" eyeglasses and look at this from a logical perspective. How can God, the creator and sustainer of the universe, and owner of the earth and everything in it, be our source and yet we *not* walk in the wealth of Abram? How can we drink from the same fountain, El Shaddai (God the Source), and not experience the level of the manifestation of God's glory that Abram experienced? Am I calling financial wealth a manifestation of the glory of God? Absolutely. It is not **the** manifestation, but you best believe it's one of them.

Solomon

You want to know an amazing fact? The richest man ever to have lived was a follower of God. His name: Solomon, king of Israel, son of David. Using biblical accounts of the amount of gold accumulated and spent by Solomon during his forty-year reign over Israel, it can be concluded that in today's economy, he would have had a total net worth of $104,129,320,296.96 at his death. That's over **$104 billion**. Carlos Slim, who recently dethroned Bill Gates as the richest man in the world, only has a net worth of about $67.8 billion. Solomon's comparative wealth was almost twice as much!

But, why was Solomon so wealthy? What was it about him that caused him to have a type of Midas touch?

> *"In Gibeon the LORD appeared to Solomon in a dream by night: and God said, Ask what I shall give thee. [6] And Solomon said, Thou hast showed unto thy servant David my father great mercy, according as he walked before thee in truth, and in righteousness, and in uprightness of heart with thee; and thou hast kept for him this great kindness, that thou hast given him a son to sit on his throne, as it is this day. [7] And now, O LORD my God, thou hast made thy servant king instead of David my father: and I am but a little child: I know not how to go out or come in. [8] And thy servant is in the midst of thy people which thou hast chosen, a great people, that cannot be numbered nor counted for multitude. [9] Give therefore thy servant an understanding heart to judge thy people, that I may discern*

between good and bad: for who is able to judge this thy so great a people? [10] And the speech pleased the Lord, that Solomon had asked this thing. [11] And God said unto him, Because thou hast asked this thing, and hast not asked for thyself long life; neither hast asked riches for thyself, nor hast asked the life of thine enemies; but hast asked for thyself understanding to discern judgment; [12] Behold, I have done according to thy words: lo, I have given thee a wise and an understanding heart; so that there was none like thee before thee, neither after thee shall any arise like unto thee. [13] And I have also given thee that which thou hast not asked, both riches, and honor: so that there shall not be any among the kings like unto thee all thy days."

1 Kings 3:5-13

The answer to our question is quite simple after reading this passage. Solomon's humble heart and God-approved priorities moved God in such a way that He promised Solomon unbelievable wisdom (which Solomon asked for) and unbelievable riches and honor (which he didn't ask for).

When you study the reign of Solomon and calculate his income and expenses over the course of his reign (as detailed in the biblical account), the only conclusion you can arrive at is that God held true to his word. Over the course of Solomon's reign, his average annual net income was 2.6 billion dollars!

Look at the reaction Solomon's contemporaries had when they witnesses his abundant wealth firsthand.

"And when the queen of Sheba heard of the fame of
Solomon concerning the name of the LORD, she came to
prove him with hard questions. [2] And she came to
Jerusalem with a very great train, with camels that bore
spices, and very much gold, and precious stones: and when
she was come to Solomon, she communed with him of all
that was in her heart. [3] And Solomon told her all her
questions: there was not any thing hid from the king, which
he told her not. [4] And when the queen of Sheba had seen
all Solomon's wisdom, and the house that he had built, [5]
And the meat of his table, and the sitting of his servants,
and the attendance of his ministers, and their apparel, and
his cupbearers, and his ascent by which he went up unto the
house of the LORD; there was no more spirit in her. [6]
And she said to the king, It was a true report that I heard
in mine own land of thy acts and of thy wisdom. [7]
Howbeit I believed not the words, until I came, and mine
eyes had seen it: and, behold, the half was not told me: thy
wisdom and prosperity exceedeth the fame which I heard."

1 Kings 10:1-7

The queen of Sheba visited Solomon after hearing of his great
fame. But, her motives were anything but pure. She intended to prove
that he wasn't all that his reputation claimed by trapping him with
difficult questions, demonstrating that he wasn't as wise as everyone
thought. Boy, was she in for a surprise.

She presented her enigmas to Solomon, who answered all her
questions. When the queen saw how wise and unbelievably wealthy

Solomon was, she had quite an amusing reaction. The fifth verse says that there was no more spirit in her, which could be interpreted a couple of ways. Either she was simply breathless at his great wealth and wisdom, or she actually fainted.

This woman set out to confound Solomon with difficult questions. She brought great wealth along with her—probably in order to impress Solomon (go figure)—but wound up presenting it as an offering to his greatness (v. 10). As a matter of fact, no one ever again presented so great a gift to Solomon. In today's dollars, her gift was worth **$87,091,200**.

Mary Magdalene

Many people are surprised to know that Mary Magdalene, the so-called prostitute (although there's absolutely no biblical proof to that effect), was a major financier of Jesus' ministry.

> *"And certain women, which had been healed of evil spirits and infirmities, Mary called Magdalene, out of whom went seven devils, And Joanna the wife of Chuza Herod's steward, and Susanna, and many others, which ministered unto him of their substance."*
>
> *Luke 8:2-3*

In this passage, Mary, Joanna, and Susanna were women who helped finance Jesus' ministry. The language of the text seems to indicate that their gifts were pretty substantial, especially when one considers that women usually weren't mentioned by name in the Bible unless they did something extraordinary. Yet here, all three of these financiers were mentioned by name, among *"many others"*. This indicates that for some reason, *their* gifts were worthy of individual mention among the many.

Jesus' Ministry & Disciples

When trying to establish that Jesus and His disciples were poor, people have very obvious passages that they must either distort or completely overlook. An honest examination of these passages leads one to the inescapable conclusion that Jesus' ministry did, in fact, have plenty of financial resources.

First of all, we should look at the livelihoods of the disciples to see if their careers would have scarcely or generously provided for them and their families (if applicable).

Peter, Andrew, James, and John were all fishermen (Matt. 4:18; Matt. 4:21). Being a fisherman wasn't necessarily a prosperous career; however, Mark 1:20 indicates that James and John's fishery was a family-owned business that employed workers. This implies that the business was a successful one, and hardly leads to the conclusion that James and John were poor.

We don't know how successful Peter's and Andrew's fishing careers were, but without this information, there's no reason to simply assume that they were poor.

Matthew was a tax collector for the Roman Empire, so there's very little reason to believe that he was poor. In fact, Luke 5:29

implies that Matthew, who was at first called Levi, was actually pretty wealthy. He held a banquet in Jesus' honor and invited a large crowd of his tax collector associates, among others.

We don't know what Philip's career was, and there's no solid biblical evidence that could be called upon to prove or disprove whether he was wealthy. One passage provides a hint of evidence to answer this question, but it's circumstantial at best.

"And there were certain Greeks among them that came up to worship at the feast: [21] The same came therefore to Philip, which was of Bethsaida of Galilee, and desired him, saying, Sir, we would see Jesus."

John 12:20-21

In this passage, Greek travelers approached Philip when they wanted to gain access to Jesus. It's possible that this could be an indication that he wasn't a poor man. One would think that Greeks would likely not approach an impoverished man to gain access to Jesus, even if he were one of Jesus' disciples. Surely, they would have more likely approached one of the wealthy sons of Zebedee instead (James and John). Again, this is not solid evidence at all, but as with Peter and Andrew, not enough information is available with which to make a solid determination one way or the other.

We don't know what Judas Iscariot's career was before becoming a disciple, but we do have enough information to conclude that he was most likely not poor. Famous for being the disciple who betrayed Jesus, Judas was the treasurer of Jesus' ministry. It wouldn't make sense for him to be the treasurer if he didn't know how to manage money.

I would have thought that Matthew, the tax collector, would have been a more obvious choice. But apparently, Jesus knew more about their individual qualifications than we do today. The fact that he knew how to handle and dispense money gives a strong indication that he was an educated man. During those days, education was a luxury that simply wasn't afforded to poor people. So, it's more likely than not that Judas wasn't poor.

Bartholomew, Thomas, James the Less (so called to distinguish him from John's brother, another disciple), Simon, and Jude are all people we don't have enough information about in order to make a determination on their financial status. As stated before, this doesn't imply that they were impoverished, just as it doesn't imply that they were wealthy. It simply means that we don't know.

Not only can we examine the careers of the disciples as an indication of their financial status, but we can also take a look at their ministry during the time of Jesus.

"And he said unto them, Take nothing for your journey,
neither staves, nor scrip, neither bread, neither money;
neither have two coats apiece."

Luke 9:3

In this passage, Jesus instructed His disciples to take along no provisions on their missionary journey. Two of the things He told them to leave behind were money and extra coats. Consider that during those days, the disciples didn't have access to ATMs or Western Union. They would have had to take along as many provisions as possible. So, considering that Jesus told them *not* to take anything along, we can deduce that they did, in fact, have enough to fund the journey. As a matter of fact, they apparently had enough money for redundant attire in their wardrobe (multiple coats).

"For some of them thought, because Judas had the bag, that Jesus had said unto him, Buy those things that we have need of against the feast; or, that he should give something to the poor."

John 13:29

Something many "poor-Jesus" fanatics fail to acknowledge is that Jesus' ministry apparently made it a habit to give to the poor. In addition, it appears that the disciples didn't consider themselves poor. They *gave* to the poor, but they themselves weren't poor. Consider their response to Jesus' warning about the dangers of riches…

"And the disciples were astonished at his words. But Jesus answereth again, and saith unto them, Children, how hard is it for them that trust in riches to enter into the kingdom of God! [25] It is easier for a camel to go through the eye of a needle, than for a rich man to enter into the kingdom of God. [26] And they were astonished out of measure, saying among themselves, Who then can be saved?"

Mark 10:24-26

Poor people would hardly have responded to Jesus' warning about riches by asking, "In that case, who *can* be saved?" On the contrary, a poor man's response would have been, "Well, thank God I'm not one of those with possessions." Apparently, they considered themselves a part of the group Jesus was warning.

> *"This he said, not that he cared for the poor; but because he was a thief, and had the bag, and bare what was put therein."*
>
> John 12:6

Although a thief, Judas was the keeper of the moneybag, the treasurer of Jesus' ministry. What's interesting is that although Judas was stealing from the ministry, they still had enough money to give to the poor, buy food (John 4:8), and pay other ministry expenses.

I don't think it takes a leap of faith to conclude that the disciples were, indeed, well off. They may or may not have been what one might consider rich or wealthy, but it's pretty obvious that they weren't anywhere near poor.

Jesus

It's nothing short of shocking that so many Christians still believe the traditional, unbiblical teaching that Jesus was a poverty-stricken man. It's clear that we've got a lot of work to do when it comes to purging false doctrines from our pulpits. Let's take a look at what the Bible shows us about Jesus' financial status.

First of all, people who defend the poor-Jesus doctrine quickly point to the fact that Jesus was born in a lowly manger with animals as bunkmates. But, according to the Bible, the conclusion that Jesus' family was poor is far from the truth.

> *"And she brought forth her firstborn son, and wrapped him in swaddling clothes, and laid him in a manger; because there was no room for them in the inn."*
>
> *Luke 2:7*

You have to ask yourself: If Joseph and Mary had no money, why did it matter that there was no room in the inn? Apparently, they *did* have money for a room, but there simply weren't any rooms available because so many had ventured back to Bethlehem for the census. Yes, Jesus was born in a manager, but that only happened because the inn was full. Had they arrived sooner, Jesus would have, no doubt, been born in the relative comfort of a private room.

> *"And when [the wise men] were come into the house, they saw the young child with Mary his mother, and fell down, and worshiped him: and when they had opened their treasures, they presented unto him gifts; gold, and frankincense, and myrrh."*
>
> *Matthew 2:11*

Notice that the wise men didn't come to the stable to see and worship Jesus. They came to the *house*. Apparently, when space finally opened up, Joseph immediately moved his family into a house, which he most likely rented until Jesus was old enough to travel safely. Consider that by the time the wise men arrived, Jesus was a "young child", not still a baby. This means that they remained in Bethlehem for some time after Jesus' birth.

But, exactly how old was Jesus when the wise men arrived? How long had He and His parents stayed in Bethlehem in this house? We find a hint when Herod questioned the wise men as they were on their way to worship Jesus.

> *"Then Herod, when he saw that he was mocked of the wise men, was exceeding wroth, and sent forth, and slew all the children that were in Bethlehem, and in all the coasts thereof, from two years old and under, according to the time which he had diligently inquired of the wise men."*
>
> *Matthew 2:16*

According to what the wise men told Herod, he had reason to believe that Jesus was at most two years old at the time he gave the order to kill the young boys in Bethlehem and the surrounding coasts. Most likely, this order went out in a matter of a few weeks after the wise men found Jesus in the house.

So, there's a strong indication that Jesus was just under 2 years old at the time the wise men arrived, meaning that his family had enough money to stay in Bethlehem for upwards of 2 years. We can certainly assume that Joseph was employed in Bethlehem during this period; yet to have relocated to Bethlehem for so long a period of time, they must have had some degree of financial padding to support themselves, especially during the first few months.

Consider also that at a moment's notice, Joseph was able to pack up his family and travel as far as Egypt when God warned him about Herod's plot (Matt. 2:13-14). A poor family could hardly have done this.

Furthermore, we can logically conclude that Jesus belonged to a middle class family, at the very least. Consider that Jesus was a descendent of the revered Davidic dynasty. He wasn't just another Jew. Also, keep in mind that His father, Joseph, was a carpenter—a trade Jesus likely went into during the missing years of His teens and twenties.

Now that we've dispelled the myth that Jesus' family was poverty-stricken, let's look at Jesus Himself. A very easy argument to make regarding Jesus financial state is that Jesus was found in the Temple teaching the teachers (Luke 2:46-47). As I stated previously, a formal education was not something that was available to the poor during those days, neither in secular nor religious studies. Obviously, His family was financially stable enough to provide a quality education for Him.

Now, don't fall into the trap of thinking that Jesus was only able to teach in the Temple because of some spontaneous burst of divine knowledge. Luke 2:52 (just a few verses after Jesus was found teaching in the Temple) states that Jesus "increased in wisdom", meaning He wasn't born with absolute knowledge. He grew into it in much the same way that we do. So again, He was apparently well educated, an indication of His family's wealth.

Many people reference Luke 9:58 in defense of their poor-Jesus position. But, let's take a look at the greater context of this verse.

> *And it came to pass, when the time was come that he should be received up, he steadfastly set his face to go to Jerusalem, [52] And sent messengers before his face: and they went, and entered into a village of the Samaritans, to make ready for him. [53] And they did not receive him, because his face was as though he would go to Jerusalem. [54] And when his disciples James and John saw this, they said, Lord, wilt thou that we command fire to come down from heaven, and consume them, even as Elijah did? [55] But he turned, and rebuked them, and said, Ye know not what manner of spirit ye are of. [56] For the Son of man is not come to destroy men's lives, but to save them. And they went to another village. [57] And it came to pass, that, as they went in the way, a certain man said unto him, Lord, I will follow thee whithersoever thou goest. [58] And Jesus said unto him, Foxes have holes, and birds of the air have nests; but the Son of man hath not where to lay his head."*
>
> *Luke 9:51-58*

My heart is made heavy when people take passages out of context in order to justify unbiblical positions. When you look at Jesus' statement that "foxes have holes...", you'll arrive at no other conclusion but that He was ***not*** saying that He was homeless. Rather, He was speaking directly in response to the fact that He was just turned away from the Samaritan village, where a place to lay His head was not given because the people rejected Him. He wasn't actually saying that He didn't *own* a place to live, but that the price of following Him was the possibility of not having somewhere to sleep because people could reject His ministry.

In fact, the Bible is *clear* on the point that Jesus **did**, in fact, have a home.

> *"Then Jesus turned, and saw them following, and saith unto them, What seek ye? They said unto him, Rabbi, (which is to say, being interpreted, Master,) where dwellest thou? [39] He saith unto them, Come and see. They came and saw where he dwelt, and abode with him that day: for it was about the tenth hour."*
>
> John 1:38-39

What does this passage show us? –That Jesus not only had a home, but He also had room for company.

But, the evidence doesn't end there. Let's look further at what the Bible says about our Lord's finances.

> *"Then the soldiers, when they had crucified Jesus, took his garments, and made four parts, to every soldier a part; and also his coat: now the coat was without seam, woven from the top throughout. [24] They said therefore among themselves, Let us not rend it, but cast lots for it, whose it shall be: that the Scripture might be fulfilled, which saith, They parted my raiment among them, and for my vesture they did cast lots.*

71

These things therefore the soldiers did."

John 19:23-24

When Jesus was crucified, His clothing was given to the soldiers, who divided His garments into four parts, one per soldier. But, when they got to His seamless coat, they left it in tact and gambled for it. Why? —Because it was too valuable to divide into pieces. So much for a poor Jesus…

When we consider these biblical examples of financially prosperous people in the Bible, including our Lord Jesus, we can conclude that it takes a greater leap of faith to believe that God *doesn't* want us financially prosperous than it would take to believe that He does. So, rejoice in the fact that God has manifested His promise in the lives of others, and that He'll do it in your life, too.

"Then Peter opened his mouth, and said,
Of a truth I perceive that God is no
respecter of persons"

Acts 10:34

Section Two

Dealing With The Drawbacks

Every doctrine in the Christian church has drawbacks. It's an unfortunate reality that we have to deal with because of the fallen state of the world. But, drawbacks do not indicate that something is not God's design or purpose. They simply indicate that anything can be corrupted if not maintained within the boundaries of God's word.

I would be quite remiss if I failed to point out the drawbacks associated with financial prosperity. One mistake many prosperity preachers make is to spend all their time energetically proclaiming the benefits of riches and wealth, all the while failing to warn people that if they take their prosperity (or pursuit thereof) to an ungodly extreme, they are doomed—both in this life, as well as the next.

So, let's take some time to bring balance to the great news we've uncovered thus far. Let's deal with the drawbacks associated with prosperity, so that we can enjoy its benefits without being caught off guard by any unexpected consequences.

4

The *Just Enough* Movement

lthough a large number of Christians are opening up to the prosperity message, many are still ardently opposed to it. For a variety of reasons, this camp generally has a singular view of the issue of prosperity, and that view is staunchly negative.

As those opposed to the prosperity message get more vocal in their attacks of prosperity preachers—and of the prosperity message in general—it seems that they have started their own de facto movement—what I call the "Just Enough" movement. While the prosperity message rests upon God's desire for us to walk in *more than enough* (the overflow of wealth, health, and success), the anti-prosperity message finds its foundation in the Christian virtues of self-denial, humility, and what they wrongly perceive as Jesus' own financial poverty.

It hurts my heart to know that so many people are so passionately opposed to the prosperity message. Many of their attacks are nothing short of hostile, and one may wonder if there isn't a bit of jealousy involved, rather than "righteous" indignation. Whatever their motivations—and I'm sure the motivations differ from person to person—it boils down to the fact that they've simply missed the mark when it comes to interpreting God's will for our finances.

A Few Valid Points

To their credit, some of the accusations these *Just Enough*ers have leveled against a few particular "prosperity preachers" are founded upon fairly good evidence that those specific individuals *are*, indeed, motivated by greed. Not only are their presentations of the prosperity message full of spiritual gimmicks (like anointed prayer cloths in exchange for a contribution), but they also craftily manipulate the good word regarding prosperity into a means of receiving more and more money from the believers.

These cases of greed and doctrinal corruption are certainly unfortunate; but should we reject the entire prosperity "barrel"— which we've already determined is founded upon biblical truths— based upon a few bad apples? Are God's promises concerning our finances unable to stand on the power of their own merits?

Ultimately, it comes as no surprise that Satan would attempt to corrupt the prosperity message, not only from the outside (by the anti-prosperity movement), but also from the inside (by corrupt preachers). I'd be lying if I said that there were not prosperity preachers out there who are motivated by greed, rather than a desire to see God's people walk in the wealth that is their promised heritage. But again, such an admission has no bearing on the veracity of the message itself.

Even having acknowledged the reality that there are greed-driven wolves in some pulpits, we must be very careful when attempting to assign such ungodly motivations to individuals. We have to consistently remind ourselves that it is not a crime to be unafraid to walk in covenant wealth, and it's certainly not a crime to teach God's word regarding that covenant. God *wants* His children to live in financial excess. We must, therefore, be especially careful when assigning motives to those who teach and/or live in this biblical manifestation of God's will.

A Misdirected Focus

I have spent a considerable amount of time examining the doctrines espoused by *Just Enough* preachers, and I can draw no conclusion but that many of those who subscribe to such a doctrine all but view wealth as a sin in and of itself, or at least as a gross misrepresentation of Christ. A substantial number of their accusations aren't based off of what the Bible actually teaches regarding wealth, but on the fact that the particular prosperity preacher is wealthy.

But, has the reality that some people unapologetically walk in God's will for their finances become evidence that such people are motivated by greed? Certainly not! Since when is experiencing God's will for one's life a damnable act of sacrilege?

Notwithstanding the fact that God desires for His children to be wealthy, we simply cannot afford to value or devalue a message of God because of the messenger who delivers it. As I stated in the

Introduction, the message is infinitely more important than the messenger.

When it comes to the doctrinal aspects of the prosperity message, passages like Proverbs 10:22, Ecclesiastes 5:19, Malachi 3:10, and Luke 6:38 clearly indicate that God has, indeed, made promises of abundant wealth and financial increase to His children. Do we choose to ignore these promises for fear of the possibility that #1) the person preaching about it may or may not be motivated by greed, or #2) the hearer's response may or may not be motivated by greed?

I answer this question by simply asking, "Was God so afraid of our potential reactions to His promises that He chose not to make them in the first place?"

It never ceases to amaze me how quickly people forget that these aren't the prosperity preacher's promises. They're God's promises; and as such, they must be taught, believed, and honored by experiencing their fulfillment in our lives.

God has not empowered us to determine which of His promises are "legitimate", and which He should have thought twice about. The Bible calls *every* gift of God both good and perfect (James 1:17). Consider that fact in light of the admission that the acquisition and enjoyment of wealth is one of God's gifts toward us (Eccl. 5:19). It doesn't take rocket science to connect the dots here. Riches and wealth *are* a gift of God, and as such, they are a **good and perfect gift**.

As a teacher of God's word, I am charged to teach the whole counsel of God, regardless of the ability of the hearers to corrupt the truths being taught. While I ***must*** attempt to preclude the possibility of doctrinal corruption by exposing the dangers of wealth, I must yet be unafraid to tell the truth, the whole truth, and nothing but the truth; and the truth is that wealth is not our enemy. We cannot sacrifice the biblical veracity of the prosperity message on the altar of good intentions. We must honor God's word enough to teach it all, ***and*** to teach it in a way that limits misapplication.

Ultimately, God's teachers and preachers must remind themselves that all God has commissioned them to do is convey to His people a balanced perspective on biblical truths. All we can do is teach it, and trust God to take care of the rest. As Paul so eloquently put it, "I have planted, Apollos watered; but God gave the increase" (1Co. 3:6).

Upon reflection, you realize that biblical prosperity isn't the only doctrine that has the ability to be corrupted by both the preacher and the hearer. Looking back in history, the doctrine of the very nature of Christ was corrupted to such a degree that the Church had to hold a council to settle the matter once and for all. So, should we stop teaching the humanity of Christ because Arianism corrupted this truth? (Arianism is the theological doctrine that espouses that Jesus Christ was a created being, not the eternal God). Should we be fearful of teaching the reality that Hell (or more properly, the lake of fire) exists as a literal place of eternal punishment just because some people have corrupted that doctrine by using fear to manipulate others? Obviously not.

The darkness brought on by the misinterpretation and misapplication of God's word regarding prosperity can never extinguish the radiance of the *right* interpretation. We must never silence the truth because of the lie. We must preach on, and let the light of the prosperity message shine throughout the dark realms of poverty and *just enough*.

What's Wrong With *Just Enough*?

From a biblical perspective, "just enough" is simply not a notion founded upon rightly divided truth. What we've discovered about God's will, word, and nature has clearly demonstrated that abundance and excess are His *modus operandi*. A *just enough* mentality restricts Him to the small box of our low expectations and lack of faith; and that's in stark opposition to His desire to give us exceeding abundantly above all that we ask our think. We have to keep in mind: He can only do exceedingly abundantly above... according to the power of faith that works within us (Eph. 3:20; Jas. 1:6-7). Where faith falters, so does God's "freedom" to accomplish His will in our lives (Matt. 13:58).

The notion that God doesn't want us to have more than what is required for comfortable, modest living is not only contrary to His revealed nature as "**More** Than Enough", but it's also quite selfish. If we have just enough resources to get by, how can we help others who are struggling; and even if we *can* help others, how much more *could* we have helped if our own financial obligations had not consumed the bulk of our resources?

We know from Romans 13:8 that God doesn't want us owing people. We're required to pay our bills. Ergo, if we have just enough to get by from week to week, where is the cheerful liberality that's supposed to characterize the Christian life (2Co. 9:7)? Sure, one may give cheerfully in small amounts and a few times per year, but that hardly demonstrates the heart of God concerning our giving.

Another major problem with *just enough* is that it limits the Body of Christ's ability to expand the Kingdom. Anti-prosperity preachers are very hesitant to acknowledge that ministry costs large amounts of money. But, this is a reality soon realized by people who become actively involved in ministry.

It amazes me how the very people who speak out against prosperity on their television and radio ministries don't have a problem begging for contributions toward the end of their broadcast. It seems to me that if people had more money, they'd *give* more, and if they *gave* more, these same anti-prosperity preachers wouldn't have to constantly request additional funding for ministry operation.

Conspiracy

> *"And have no fellowship with the unfruitful works of*
> *darkness, but rather expose them."*
>
> *Eph. 5:11*

Some time ago, I preached a message entitled "Conspiracy". It dealt with a nefarious plot Satan's kingdom has devised in order to make the Body of Christ impotent to deal with the realities of spiritual warfare. As I was mapping out the content of this book, I found it absolutely essential that I include a section about a second conspiracy, one that deals specifically with our finances, and with the primary purpose of wealth we discovered in Chapter 2.

You have to understand a very important point here. There are ultimately only two kingdoms in existence, only two high powers: the kingdom of Light and the kingdom of darkness. There is no in-between. Something either advances God's kingdom or Satan's. So, when spiritual territory belongs to God, it doesn't belong to Satan. When it belongs to Satan, it is not under God's domain (although it is still under His divine Providential rulership).

That being said, it stands to reason that Satan is not satisfied to sit back while the kingdom of God is advanced throughout the world. Every soul that truly makes Jesus Lord is a loss to Satan's kingdom. So, it's illogical to assume that Satan will sit idly by and lose territory as the glorious message of the gospel is taken to the ends of the earth.

Far from being passive in his reaction to the Church's attack on his domain, Satan actively works to quell the advance of the Kingdom of God. Not only has he directly attacked the ability of the Church to advance the Kingdom from the outside—social secularism, political liberalism, and other anti-Christ ideologies—but he has also conspired more closely to home by working *within* the Church to cause the Church to limit its own ability to advance the Kingdom. How? –Put simply, by advancing the anti-prosperity movement.

You see, a wise—or shall I say, devious—adversary won't focus solely on attacking an opponent from the outside. If he can infiltrate the enemy's domain and attack from the inside (even if only indirectly), that can serve his purposes much better than any frontal attack. Unfortunately, Satan has near mastered this tactic.

It's interesting to note that while the gates of Hell shall not prevail against the Church (Matt. 16:18), She *can* be naive and immature enough to allow the gates of Hell to work within Her own borders, causing Her to prevail against Her own self (Matt. 12:25). Seeing this weakness, Satan has devised and implemented a battle plan to infiltrate the Church and stir up doctrinal strife and contention. Just do an Internet search on "prosperity preacher" and you'll see that a vast majority of the search results are negative websites run *by* Christians *against* Christians. These people constantly bash both the prosperity message and prosperity preachers, and—taking direction from Eph. 5:11 (quoted previously)—I want to show you *why* this is happening.

The financial resources of the Church are derived from those who comprise Her. When the members of a local congregation are fairly poor, the Church has very limited resources with which to fund ministry operations, meaning that Her reach and effectiveness is hindered, albeit not non-existent. Many facets of ministry do require a lot of money, and a congregation with strained resources simply cannot undertake such activities, even though the need in a given area may be great.

So, by keeping the Body of Christ from experiencing the fullness of God's covenant of wealth, Satan is actually limiting, albeit not canceling, our ability to advance the Kingdom. Many people may not want to make such an admission, but it's the truth nonetheless.

Let's examine the inner workings of this battle plan, this conspiracy to attack the Church from the inside. According to Matt.

9:29, 13:58, and James 1:6-7, faith is an essential component of receiving. In fact, Hebrews 11:6 emphatically declares that it's *impossible* to please God without it. Knowing how vital faith is to manifestation, a sincere person's response would be: How can I have faith, and more of it?

> *"So then faith cometh by hearing, and hearing by the word*
> *of God."*
>
> Romans 10:17

Faith is both conceived and nurtured by the word of God. It's important to understand, however, that this is not just *any* word, but the word that pertains to the specific area you're looking to build faith in. For instance, faith in God as a healer isn't built simply by reading a genealogy in the Bible. However, when you hear and believe God's promises concerning health and healing, your faith in that specific area *can* and *will* be increased.

When it comes to financial prosperity, Satan understands better than most how to keep people from seeing wealth manifested in their lives. By keeping believers from hearing the word of God on the matter, he's able to unravel the fabric of biblical prosperity in the lives of God's people.

What's so unfortunate about this conspiracy is that we've allowed it to work rather well. The Church routinely and almost reflexively challenges the prosperity message, and often drags the names of prosperity preachers through the mud. In response, preachers and teachers have shied away from the subject altogether, or they tread very carefully, fearing to go into the depth you're getting in this book.

I've been more of a "whole counsel of God" teacher myself, and I truly thank God for that conviction. He has delivered me from the opinions of people, and given me a desire to teach His truth, no matter how unpopular.

I sincerely pray that God delivers those who carry His message from the fear of people's response! We must start valuing God's people enough to preach the word in season and out of season, because if 1,000 people reject it and two receive it, it was worth the effort.

If I teach financial prosperity and 80% reject it, I've still advanced the Kingdom. But, if I choose not to teach it *because* of the 80%, **nobody gets helped**. Shame on us, the preachers and teachers of the word! And shame on us, the Christians who always think a prosperity message is coming from a crook who wants nothing more than to steal our money.

It's time to turn Satan's conspiracy inside out and teach this message with boldness and conviction. Who cares how many news programs attack us? To hell with the opinions of men. Let God arise, and let His enemies be scattered (Ps. 68:1). It's better for us to fear and serve God rather than man! (Luke 12:4-5; Acts 5:29)

The Body of Christ is making a serious impact in the world today. But, think of how much further along we'd be if the wealth of the sinner was *in the hands of the just*, rather than simply being "laid up" for us (Prov. 13:22)? If more Christians consistently walked in biblical prosperity, we could have accomplished so much more by now.

But, yesterday's gone. It's time for us to make a decision *today* to walk in the wealth that is our promised inheritance, and whoever doesn't like it… too bad.

The Doctrinal Errors

The *Just Enough* movement is not only an ideological movement opposed to Christian prosperity. It actually finds its basis in the text of the Scriptures. However, *everything* is in the interpretation, and that's exactly where the *Just Enough* preachers fall short.

When attempting to discern God's will as it pertains to our finances, it doesn't suffice to simply find something in the Scriptures that validates one position or another. Bible passages were not written in a vacuum, and must be interpreted in the light of two very important things: 1) their immediate context, and 2) the overall, sure and certain teachings of the Scriptures.

I'm the first to admit that anti-prosperity preachers can take you to Scripture in order to validate their positions. But, the reality is that Scripture can be used to validate all sorts of untrue positions. Such is what we call "twisting the Scriptures". Whether wittingly or unwittingly, the result is the same—misinterpretation and misapplication.

Let's examine some of the passages anti-prosperity preachers commonly use to justify their disagreement with the prosperity message.

"For it is easier for a camel to go through a needle's eye,
than for a rich man to enter into the kingdom of God."

Luke 18:25

This is probably the most commonly referenced passage anti-prosperity preachers use to refute the prosperity message. I really think that's a shame, because if people would just take the time to read the next two verses (and to read the previous six verses), they'd get a much clearer picture of what Jesus was actually saying.

Upon examining the context of Jesus' statement, we discover a very important point. The statement was made in direct response to the fact that a well-intentioned young man was not willing to part with his wealth in order to be Jesus' disciple. Notice that Jesus made this statement after seeing that the young man was "very sorrowful" (v. 24a).

This is important to establish because it shows us that Jesus' entire purpose for telling the man to sell all that he had and give it to the poor was not to condemn wealth, but to demonstrate to this man and all those around that if they want to be true and faithful disciples, nothing can mean more to them than following Him.

This point is in perfect keeping with Jesus' admonition that true and faithful disciples can't even prefer close family above Him (Lk. 14:26). Must we consider this admonition as a condemnation of family? Of course not. Neither should we consider Luke 18:25 a condemnation of wealth.

One of the traps wealthy people fall into is treasuring their wealth, rather than the Giver of it. But, if wealth is not a stumbling block to some, there's no biblical justification for believing that God is against their financial excess.

Notice that when the disciples responded in desperation to Jesus' statement, asking who could be saved if a rich man could scarcely enter the kingdom of God, Jesus answered, "With men this is impossible; but with God all things are possible." It's interesting to note what Jesus *didn't* say. He *didn't* say, "Well, that's exactly why God doesn't want you rich!" To the contrary, He basically said, "That's why you need to keep your eyes on God, and make sure not to make the mistake this young man just made."

The apostle Paul makes this very point in 1Timothy 6:17, saying, "Charge them that are rich in this world, that they be not highminded; nor trust in uncertain riches, but in the living God…" Paul didn't say to charge the rich to give away their wealth, but simply to take care not to treasure it.

These warnings do not imply God's will one way or the other. They simply serves as warnings, and very necessary ones. Both Paul and Jesus' point is simple: If you're rich, make sure that you never exalt that wealth above God. To that I say, "Amen and amen!"

This brings me to another passage commonly used to refute the prosperity message: Matthew 6:19-21.

> "*Lay not up for yourselves treasures upon earth, where moth and rust doth corrupt, and where thieves break through and steal: [20] But lay up for yourselves treasures in heaven, where neither moth nor rust doth corrupt, and where thieves do not break through nor steal: [21] For where your*

treasure is, there will your heart be also."

As with the previous admonitions, Jesus reminded us here that we ought not store treasures for ourselves in this life. Unfortunately, misguided people interpret this to mean that those with wealth are in violation of this warning. But, are they?

What *Just Enough* people fail to realize is that money is not, in itself, a treasure. Have you ever heard the statement, *One man's trash is another man's treasure?* Well, that statement demonstrates a very important point. Something is not a treasure until it's *treasured.* You can be rich and not *treasure* money and material possessions (even though you may have them in abundance), and you can also be poor and treasure what you *don't* have—coveting others' possessions.

So, yet again, we don't find a condemnation of wealth in Matt. 6:19-21. We simply find another important warning regarding what we hold as treasures in our eyes.

Rich or poor, your treasure must be the Lord Jesus. I'm reminded of the lyrics to a song of worship I love. It says that the Lord is more precious than silver, more costly than gold, more beautiful than diamonds, and beyond comparison with anything desired in life. Contrary to what anti-prosperity advocates believe, you *can* be rich and still feel that way about the Lord. And going back to Luke 18:18-27, we must always be willing to part with our riches (in part or in whole) should God command so.

This passage is closely related to yet another that is commonly used to lead people away from God's promises regarding wealth.

"No man can serve two masters: for either he will hate the one, and love the other; or else he will hold to the one, and despise the other. Ye cannot serve God and mammon."

Matt. 6:24

The term "mammon" refers to riches, and is commonly personified as a false god or devil in various translations. But, whether mammon is simply a general reference to riches or a literal devil isn't as important as the point Jesus was making in this passage.

Jesus taught that if we desire to be servants of God, we cannot be servants of our riches (or lack thereof). When making decisions, financial considerations must never outweigh the word and will of God. We simply cannot serve God and money, because oftentimes, God will require something of us that our economics won't agree with. Such was certainly the case with the rich young ruler, who wasn't willing to part with his wealth in order to follow Jesus.

So, Jesus' point is not only valid; it's *vital.* It's especially important that wealthy Christians allow God to occupy an unchallenged position of priority and authority in their lives. If money—or any other thing—ever usurps this sovereign authority, they'll be on very dangerous ground—for no one can faithfully serve two masters, nor will God tolerate such a thing (Ex. 20:3).

The problem anti-prosperity preachers have in their interpretation of this passage is that they take Jesus' words as a condemnation of riches; but there is absolutely no legitimate justification for interpreting His words in such a fashion. No one can serve two masters. That fact is absolutely true. However, as long as you don't make money an authority in your life (a *master*), you're not serving two masters. Notice that Jesus didn't say that you couldn't have riches, but that you couldn't *serve* riches. There's a difference, and this is where *Just Enough*ers miss the mark.

The anti-prosperity camp is notorious for misapplying and misinterpreting the Scriptures. In fact, they *have* to have this problem; otherwise, they wouldn't be anti-prosperity (especially considering that God Himself is *pro*-prosperity).

One of the most blatant misinterpretations I've ever come across was a reference to Psalm 73:12.

> *"Behold, these are the ungodly, who prosper in the world;*
> *they increase in riches."*

In that he quoted this passage in defense of an anti-prosperity position, the *Just Enough*er obviously believed that all those who are rich (or *increase* in riches) are ungodly. In his mind, this passage was stating that those who prosper in the world are not in God's will. Thankfully, it actually says nothing of the sort.

First of all, such a conclusion would be an indictment against every wealthy person of God in the Scriptures—from Abraham to Isaac; from Boaz to Solomon; from Mary Magdalene to Joseph of Arimathea. But, it would also be an indictment against God Himself, considering that it is **He** who promised to give us "power to get wealth" (Deut. 8:18). Shame on Jehovah (if these anti-prosperity people are right)!

91

While we're on the subject, why are wealth and riches (which supposedly characterize ungodliness) in the house of those who fear the Lord, and those who delight in His commandments (Ps. 112:1-3)? By this interpretation, shouldn't wealth and riches rather be in the house of those who *disobey* the Lord?

It's obvious that David was not making a doctrinal statement in Psalm 73:12, but was rather speaking to the reality that he was witnessing in his particular situation. He saw ungodly people prospering, and he recorded his frustrations at such a reality. I'm sure that if we look around the world we live in, we can easily see the same thing. But, does that mean that prosperity is a *bad* thing? I also see ungodly people with healthy bodies. Does that mean that God must want us sick?

> *"Perverse disputings of men of corrupt minds, and destitute of the truth, supposing that gain is godliness: from such withdraw thyself."*
>
> 1 Timothy 6:5

This is yet another passage very commonly used to dispute the prosperity doctrine, and in some ways, it does serve as an indictment of some prosperity preachers. As I dealt with previously, doctrinal corruptions exist within every biblical school of thought. Unfortunately, the prosperity doctrine is not exempt.

Some preachers teach that financial gain is a means to godliness. While they are right, in a certain sense, they fail to clearly establish this sense, showing how such a teaching is not a contradiction to 1Ti. 6:5.

This passage is absolutely true (as all biblical passages are). Gain is *not* godliness. Those who believe so fall into a very dangerous trap, supposing that their material and financial wealth has put them in a better position with God. Such a teaching exalts the acquisition of wealth and riches to a level of spiritual empowerment that is simply not supported by Scripture.

Put simply, the rich do not have an edge over the poor when it comes to godliness or one's standing with God. Rich or poor, we must all pray. Wealthy or broke, we must all fast. We're all in the same boat. We're all in desperate need of God's grace, and we all desperately need His help to keep us from going to one extreme or another when it comes to our finances.

I've personally heard some misguided teachers make the error of viewing wealth as a sign of spiritual maturity, empowerment, or a stamp of God's approval. IT IS NOT. I've even heard a few preachers tell congregations that if someone is preaching to them about wealth, they should check that preacher's suit, and if it doesn't look new and crisp, they shouldn't listen. They've taught that if a preacher is not wealthy himself, no one should accept what he has to say concerning the prosperity message. This is a grave error, and it sheds a bad doctrinal light on the prosperity message.

The church may Amen such statements, thinking that a person's status validates the message he preaches; but that doesn't make it right. Such would certainly be sage advise in the world's system; however, when it comes to the Scriptures, the message is always more important than the messenger. A whore can tell me that fornication is a sin. Her whoring doesn't make what she said untrue. A bum off of the street can preach a prosperity message. As long as he's coming from the rightly-divided word of truth, what he says shouldn't be ignored.

I reject the doctrinal error that some of my fellow prosperity preachers have made in exalting the status of the messenger. We are all God's instruments, rich and poor, and neither has a spiritual advantage. While the rich certainly have an edge in terms of *natural* empowerment (how their natural resources can be used to advance ministry), wealth itself is not a spiritual empowerment. Believing or teaching such is a serious error.

Now, this section is entitled *The Doctrinal Errors*, and thus far, it doesn't seem like the anti-prosperity movement missed it on their interpretation and application of 1Ti. 6:5. But, I referenced this passage as a doctrinal error of the *Just Enough* movement for a good reason. From a perspective quite different than the one I've just dealt with, financial gain is, in fact, godly, unlike *Just Enough*ers believe.

Anything that is a manifestation of God's will is godly. Otherwise, we'd have to conclude that the will of God itself is ungodly. Now, we've already firmly established that it's God's will for His people to be wealthy. That being the case, we can form a sure and certain conclusion. Riches and wealth, when acquired through and by means that are in keeping with God's word, is godly. Our prosperity is pleasing to God (Ps. 35:27), and as such, it is **not** a bad thing.

The Scriptures clearly warn of wealth, but they do not warn *against* wealth. This is an important distinction that the anti-prosperity people fail to make. In doing so, their interpretations conflict with

94

what the Scriptures clearly teach about God's will for our finances. He empowers us to get wealth, and teaches us to profit (Deut. 8:18; Is. 48:17). Why would He do this if wealth were evil? His blessing produces riches, not mere sufficiency (Prov. 10:22). So, is His blessing just a curse in disguise? *Just Enough*ers apparently think so.

This is where the anti-prosperity movement has it wrong. They won't usually say it explicitly, but their doctrines ultimately lead to the incorrect conclusion that wealth and gain, and those who seek such, are ungodly, plain and simple. But, how can it ever be ungodly to seek something that is clearly God's will for our lives? We should be adamant in condemning ungodly motivations, but not in condemning wealth altogether (or the godly pursuit of it).

Plenty of other doctrinal and interpretational errors exist within the *Just Enough* movement. But, rather than attempt to do an exhaustive exposition into this contrary doctrine, suffice it to say that you should not allow those voices to outweigh the rightly divided word of God, and the revelation regarding your finances that it brings. *Just Enough*ers will certainly be able to point to passages that *seem* to contradict the prosperity doctrine, but be careful not to be moved out of place by a surface-level reading of the text. Examine the context, and prayerfully determine the application of such verses. Only then can you know that you're not being tossed to and fro and every wind of doctrine (Eph. 4:14), but that you're stable in His word, seeking not a doctrine that *seems* right (Prov. 14:12), but that which *is* right.

The same warning must apply to prosperity doctrines, as well. The unfortunate truth is that some prosperity preachers *are* interested only in personal gain. So, always let the word of God being the determining factor in what you will and will not believe. You can't go wrong when you simply let God speak for Himself. Let the message preached only serve to motivate you to confirm that what was preached is actually true. (Acts 17:11)

Ultimately, the Bible is quite clear about God's intentions for our finances, and *just enough* in no way describes those intentions.

"Study [be diligent] to show thyself
approved unto God, a workman that
needeth not to be ashamed, rightly
dividing the word of truth."

2Timothy 2:15

5

The Dangers of Wealth

lthough we've established that it's God's will for us to have exceeding abundance in our finances, I can't leave it there. I must warn you of the very real and present dangers that surround the wealthy place. It's wonderful to have the blinders taken off and finally realize that God wants you rich, but it's vitally important that you have a biblical balance in this regard; otherwise, you're destined to fall victim to the snares of which the Scriptures so fervently warn.

Many of the passages warning of these *wealth snares* are the very passages anti-prosperity preachers use to refute the prosperity doctrine. What you will soon see, however, is that these passages were not intended as indictments against wealth. To the contrary, they were intended to provide balance to this serious issue, so that the adversary would not be able to take something intended as a gift of God and corrupt it like he's done so many other things.

Unfortunately, many well-intentioned Christians repeatedly misinterpret these passages, believing them to speak of wealth itself as a bad thing. Then, they turn around and propagate these errors, teaching them as absolute truths, even to the extent of personally attacking those who *do* unashamedly walk in wealth. Ultimately, they cause masses of people to reject God's good will for their finances. What a tragedy.

Now, while you may understand that these passages are warnings and not condemnations, you still must recognize that they are, indeed, warnings. You don't want to fall into the same trap on the opposite end of the doctrinal spectrum—emphasizing prosperity to the point that you single-mindedly become a pursuer of wealth, all the while forgetting that wealth is not simply for personal enjoyment, but primarily for Kingdom advancement.

"Perverse disputings of men of corrupt minds, and destitute of the truth, supposing that gain is godliness: from such withdraw thyself. [6] But godliness with contentment is great gain. [7] For we brought nothing into this world, and it is certain we can carry nothing out. [8] And having food and raiment let us be therewith content. [9] But they that will be rich fall into temptation and a snare, and into many foolish and hurtful lusts, which drown men in destruction and perdition. [10] For the love of money is the root of all evil: which while some coveted after, they have erred from the faith, and pierced themselves through with many sorrows.

[11] But thou, O man of God, flee these things; and follow

after righteousness, godliness, faith, love, patience,

meekness."

1 Timothy 6:5-11

In the previous chapter, we dealt with the reality that financial gain does not establish a person's godliness. The wealthy are not closer to God, nor are they given special consideration in the Kingdom. But, I'd like to take this a step further by looking more at the context surrounding this revelation.

The sixth verse shows us that gain is not godliness, but godliness *is* gain—and great gain, at that. When a person is consumed with the pursuit of wealth, he is no longer useful to God, because his decisions and actions are almost always filtered through the corrupt thinking resulting from such a pursuit.

Simply getting rich should not be the goal of the faithful Christian (Prov. 28:20). Verse 11 explains what we *should* be seeking is righteousness, godliness, faith, love, patience, and meekness. These are the virtues that describe a faithful Christian, not wealth.

What is God's will for our finances in light of this passage? Should we not pursue wealth at all? While some would answer with a quick no, I must both agree and disagree with that assertion.

We shouldn't pursue wealth as a driving force in our lives. It should never be the deciding factor in anything we do, and our perception of wealth should never rise above the level of it simply being a tool useful for Kingdom advancement and for living. But, having said that, we need not *fear* wealth. It is not, in itself, evil, neither is it necessarily good.

Notice that in 1Timothy 6:10 (quoted above), it is not money that is the root of all evil, as many anti-prosperity people often claim. It is the *love* of money that is the root of all evil. Money itself is neither good, nor bad. The *relationship* we have toward it is, however.

So then, verse 9 is not condemning everyone who wants to be rich, but only those who want it because of their own personal greed and ambition. If our desire is to be pleasing to God (Ps. 35:27b), and to advance His kingdom through the riches that the blessing produces (Prov. 10), we need not believe that we are ungodly.

Having said that, we must remain ever-mindful of the warning of 1Ti. 6, lest we fall into a snare. God wrote this warning because He loves us and doesn't want us deceived by riches. So, while I certainly won't tell you that it's wrong to want to be rich, I *will* tell you that if all you're trying to do is fulfill the lust of the flesh (wanting what *feels* good), the lust of the eyes (wanting what *looks* good), and/or the pride of life (wanting to exalt self in the eyes of yourself and others), you've got a serious problem. (1Jn. 2:16)

> *"Trust not in oppression, and become not vain in robbery: if*
> *riches increase, set not your heart upon them."*
>
> *Psalms 62:10*

In this Psalm, David warns us that if riches increase in our lives, we must take care not to set our hearts upon them. This really mirrors what Jesus taught in Matt. 6:19-20, commanding us to "lay not up for [ourselves] treasures" in this world.

Anti-prosperity preachers make the huge mistake of equating wealth with treasure. They assume that if a person is wealthy (or seeks wealth) that they are violating Jesus' words in Matt. 6. However, this is an interpretational mistake.

An increase in riches does not mean that the riches are actually treasured by an individual. Something is not a treasure until it is highly esteemed. In this Psalm, David showed this distinction perfectly. Riches can increase without actually becoming a treasure in the heart of a believer. Only when someone *views* riches as a treasure have they failed to maintain the proper relationship with their money.

> *"Thus saith the LORD, Let not the wise man glory in his wisdom, neither let the mighty man glory in his might, let not the rich man glory in his riches"*
>
> *Jeremiah 9:23*

It's very important as you increase more and more in riches that you never fall into the trap of glorying in those riches. As I have stated multiple times through this work, riches are nothing more than a tool for Kingdom building. It does not give you any extra points with God. As we discovered previously, riches are not a means to godliness or special favor with the Lord. Glory in *Him*, for He alone is the true source of all good things, not riches (1Ti. 6:17). In fact, if we read on to the next verse (Jer. 9:24), God says this very thing.

> *"But let him that glorieth glory in this, that he understandeth and knoweth me, that I am the LORD*

which exercise lovingkindness, judgment, and righteousness,
in the earth: for in these things I delight, saith the LORD."

The man who glories in anything but the Lord exalts that thing *above* the Lord. Knowing that every good and perfect gift comes not from riches, but from *above* (James 1:17), how can any other conclusion be drawn but that those who glory in anything other than God have stolen His glory—glory that He deserves both in His nature and in His wonderful works.

It is by God's grace alone that we have what we have, and we should **never** lose sight of that fact—especially considering that riches have a way of sprouting wings and flying away (Prov. 23:5)! If we make the mistake of glorying in riches rather than in the Lord, we'll soon find ourselves disappointed when the thing we're exalting reveals itself to be unstable and fleeting.

Never forget that "pride goes before destruction, and a haughty spirit before a fall" (Prov. 16:18). When you exalt riches (or self), you're just setting yourself up for failure.

As God explained in Jer. 9:24, riches cannot acquire the things that matter most—God's lovingkindness, judgment, and righteousness. Remain humble, and always look to Him as your source, no matter how wealthy you become, and no matter how many things you acquire in life.

"And, behold, one came and said unto him, Good Master,
what good thing shall I do, that I may have eternal life?
[17] And he said unto him, Why callest thou me good?

there is none good but one, that is, God: but if thou wilt

enter into life, keep the commandments. [18] He saith unto

him, Which? Jesus said, Thou shalt do no murder, Thou

shalt not commit adultery, Thou shalt not steal, Thou shalt

not bear false witness, [19] Honor thy father and thy

mother: and, Thou shalt love thy neighbor as thyself. [20]

The young man saith unto him, All these things have I kept

from my youth up: what lack I yet? [21] Jesus said unto

him, If thou wilt be perfect, go and sell that thou hast, and

give to the poor, and thou shalt have treasure in heaven: and

come and follow me. [22] But when the young man heard

that saying, he went away sorrowful: for he had great

possessions. [23] Then said Jesus unto his disciples, Verily I

say unto you, That a rich man shall hardly enter into the

kingdom of heaven. [24] And again I say unto you, It is

easier for a camel to go through the eye of a needle, than for a

rich man to enter into the kingdom of God. [25] When his

disciples heard it, they were exceedingly amazed, saying,

Who then can be saved? [26] But Jesus beheld them, and

said unto them, With men this is impossible; but with God

all things are possible."

Matthew 19:16-26

The portion of this passage that speaks as a warning to us about riches is verses 23-24, and anti-prosperity preachers often quote those passages to demonstrate how ungodly riches are. If we were to consider those two verses in isolation, we'd have no choice but to agree with that interpretation; however, it's a completely incorrect interpretation.

When we consider the entire context in which Jesus expressed this warning about riches, a few things immediately become clear. First of all, Jesus didn't tell the young ruler to sell all of His belongings because He hated riches. He told Him to do that because He knew that for this individual, riches were a stumbling block. Jesus saw how the man thought in his own eyes that he was a-ok spiritually, but he most certainly wasn't. He wasn't willing to part with his money, and that was what Jesus was showing him.

So, it was in immediate reaction to this that Jesus asked, "How hardly shall they that have riches enter into the kingdom of God?" Now, the Kingdom of God isn't Heaven. It's the state of God's direct authority and rulership. When we submit to God's will, we *enter* into His kingdom.

This rich young ruler didn't enter in because even though God meant a lot to him, his riches meant more. But, that certainly doesn't apply to every wealthy person. You can be filthy rich and still submissive to God's word and will. While Jesus recognized that being rich can certainly be a stumbling block in some people's lives, He was not, in any way, stating that rich people *couldn't* enter the Kingdom. Notice that He ultimately stated, "With God, it's still possible."

Now, the eye of the needle was not referring to the sowing needles we use today. The term referred to a low gate through which animals would pass in order to go out to pasture. They would have to stoop down in order to pass through it. Because a camel has a hump, passing through the needle's eye would be particularly difficult to do, though not impossible.

Ultimately, Jesus was warning that riches could make it harder to continue to submit to God. People with a lot of money can fall into the trap of treasuring their money, and if they're not willing to part with it at the Lord's word, they've got a problem. Remember, whatever's not submitted to God's rulership is not fully brought into the Kingdom. That's the point Jesus was making—not that rich Christians must give away all of their money to the poor in order to enter the Kingdom, but that rich Christians must take care to always submit to God's will, even at the expense of personal wealth.

Money is a tool, and an abundance of it is not a bad thing. The more you have, the more access you have to various resources that will aid in your Kingdom-building endeavors. However, you must never allow money to become a stumbling block in your life. The moment it becomes more than a tool, it becomes a problem. So, riches and wealth are not bad things; but only you can decide if you can actually handle the wealth that is stored up for you. (Prov. 13:22)

*"There is that maketh himself rich, yet hath nothing: there
is that maketh himself poor, yet hath great riches."*

Proverbs 13:7

The biggest danger associated with wealth, and the point that I'd like to emphasize as I bring this chapter to a close, is that greed must be rejected whenever it attempts to rear its ugly head. We **must** be wise enough to admit that when dealing with great wealth, there will, in fact, be times when we will be tempted by the luxuries associated with abundance. We must acknowledge this reality and prepare ourselves to actively resist these inherent temptations.

Anyone who disagrees with the reality that riches bring unique temptations into people's lives is only deceiving himself (Gal. 6:3) and has likely already succumbed to greed. The Bible clearly expresses the fact that riches, by their very nature, invoke certain ungodly temptations (1Ti. 6:9). That's just the way it is.

So, be wise. Remain ever-conscious of these temptations, and always take care to ensure that you do not yield to them (Gal. 6:1). You shouldn't be *satisfied* with lack, but you also must not be motivated to get rich out of a spirit of covetousness. Strive for better, but even before you get to the wealthy place, be content in whatever the state you find yourself. (Ph. 4:11; 1Ti. 6:8; Heb. 13:5)

Ultimately, all the money in the world isn't worthy to be compared to the treasure of and in Heaven. Jesus put it this way: "What shall it profit a man, if he shall gain the whole world, and lose his own soul?" (Mark 8:36)

Having substance in this temporary life isn't what's most important—not by a long shot. If our substance becomes a stumbling block to what is infinitely more valuable—our walk with God and our eternal life—it should be avoided like the plague... even given away (Matt. 19:21).

That being said—and this is important so pay attention—wealth should only be avoided by people to whom it is a stumbling block. If financial excess won't turn you from submission to God in all things, particularly in matters of finance, you shouldn't be afraid of it, and you most certainly should not deny it a place in your life.

The key is to simply be honest with yourself. As a human

being, God gave you a unique ability among all creatures—introspection and self-judgment (1Co. 11:31). If you can just be honest enough to admit that wealth would do you more harm than good, you can save yourself a life of anguish, and an eternity of damnation (Matt. 19:23). So, examine yourself, and determine whether wealth would be too dangerous for you to walk in. While this certainly won't apply to every believer, I take my hat off to those who can admit that it does, unfortunately, apply to them.

"Because thou sayest, I am rich, and increased with goods, and have need of nothing; and knowest not that thou art wretched, and miserable, and poor, and blind, and naked: [18] I counsel thee to buy of me gold tried in the fire, that thou mayest be rich; and white raiment, that thou mayest be clothed, and that the shame of thy nakedness do not appear; and anoint thine eyes with eye salve, that thou mayest see."

Revelation 3:17-18

6

Broad Is The Road… To Lack

Poverty and lack is, in my opinion, the most evil condition that exists this side of hell. It seems like everybody wants to be politically correct, but I think the truth is much better than the outright lie we've allowed to infiltrate our society—that it's okay to be poor. The truth is that there's nothing noble about being poor, and God wants better for His people.

Liberal ideologues have glorified poverty and given the poor a type of super-status in our society, but I think that we do a great disservice to the indigent when we don't let them know that God will help them rise from that condition (and without the government's help, too).

Not every Christian would consider himself/herself impoverished, but most would have to admit to a state of financial lack. Unfortunately, it's become a normal part of life for many. But contrary to traditional views, there's nothing godly about being in lack. In fact, it's a horrible place to be. Trust me, I know.

But, before we can overcome lack, we need to understand how it operates. Thankfully, the Scriptures teach us the types of decisions and lifestyles that lead to lack. Let's examine what they have to say so that we'll know what *not* to do as we're pursuing prosperity.

Lack Inducer #1: Refusal of Instruction

"Poverty and shame shall be to him that refuseth instruction: but he that regardeth reproof shall be honored."

Proverbs 13:18

One of the biggest contributors to the poverty-driven life is the refusal of instruction. I've seen it time and time again. When people refuse to listen to God's wisdom, they always fail.

The last thing you want to do is make up your mind as to what you will and won't do despite the arguments presented to the contrary. Always be open to other perspectives. It doesn't mean you're wrong, but the reality is you *could* be.

I never cease to be amazed when people seek out godly instruction as a mere formality, even though they've already decided what they're going to do. Then, after they've made a mess of things, they want prayer and fasting on their behalf. Let me be clear—**never** reject what the word of God says, no matter how obvious an alternative course of action may seem.

"There is a way which seemeth right unto a man, but the
end thereof are the ways of death."

Proverbs 14:12

Always submit to God's absolute wisdom. It's the only sure way to produce success in your life. Now, this doesn't mean that things won't get tougher in the immediate future after following God's word, but the end shall still be greater than the beginning.

Lack Inducer #2: Wrong Friendships and Associations

We've all heard the adage: "If you lay down with dogs, you'll get up with fleas." But, did you realize that this was a biblical principle, and one that leads to poverty and lack?

"He that tilleth his land shall have plenty of bread: but he
that followeth after vain persons shall have poverty enough."

Proverbs 28:19

For some odd reason, people are naturally drawn to the wrong kinds of associations. How many friendships or associations have you had in your life that you quickly learned to regret? We must make better decisions when it comes to who we call friend, or even when it comes to who we waste time associating with.

In Amos 3:3, the Bible asks the question, "Can two walk together, except they be agreed?" The implied answer is that they can't.

If you're striving to be holy, you need to surround yourself with others who are doing the same. If you want to walk in financial prosperity, stop hanging around people who aren't trying to excel. The sad reality is that in many cases, before you can pull them up, they'll tear you down. So, protect the value of what God has put on the inside of you by maintaining helpful associations.

"Don't be deceived! Evil companionships corrupt good morals."

1 Corinthians 15:33 (WEB)

If you find that you have worthless friends, this will, undoubtedly, be a very difficult lack inducer for you to shake. It's difficult to cut ties with people who have been such an active part of your life for years. But, you simply need to make the decision that where you're headed (the wealthy place) is simply not compatible with every type of association. If you want to arrive to and remain in the wealthy place, you must make the tough choices.

Now, the people you cut off will almost always be of the type who won't understand why you have to do what you have to do. They will likely not support your decision. They'll try to make you feel bad... They'll call you holier-than-thou... They'll talk about you behind your back... Just be prepared, and remind yourself that the world is bigger than the few people you may need to cut out of your life. You'll make new friends. Value your destiny more than your present associations!

Lack Inducer #3: Addictive Behavior

We all recognize drugs as an addictive and destructive behavior, but what many people don't realize is that there are many addictive behaviors that are destructive, behaviors that have nothing to do with substance abuse.

> "For the drunkard and the glutton shall come to poverty:
> and drowsiness shall clothe a man with rags."
>
> Proverbs 23:21

In referring to a drunkard and a glutton, this passage is really referring to addictive behavior in general. The two terms are only examples of *types* of addictive behavior, but I think the passage implies a condemnation of all types of addition.

It's never okay to be so drawn to a thing or behavior that it overrides your better judgment. Overeating, being a drunk, gambling, using illegal drugs, watching pornography, and even being unable to restrain from taking prescription drugs all have the power to lead you into poverty and should be avoided.

Lack Inducer #4: Laziness

> "Love not sleep, lest thou come to poverty; open thine eyes,
> and thou shalt be satisfied with bread."
>
> Proverbs 20:13

Laziness is probably the surest way to poverty and lack. If you want to produce wealth in your life, you need to understand what it means to be a hard worker, one who commits to completing a task.

It's bad enough that we sleep up to one-third of our lives away. We can't afford to sleep any more time away, nor can we afford to lounge around when there are so many things to be done. Don't misunderstand. Downtime is a very important asset, but it should not be overdone.

> *"He becometh poor that dealeth with a slack hand: but the hand of the diligent maketh rich."*
>
> *Proverbs 10:4*

It's true. Hard work pays off. When you are lazy, on the other hand, you're actully working hard to produce poverty in your life.

Lack Inducer #5: Revelry

> *"He that loveth pleasure shall be a poor man: he that loveth wine and oil shall not be rich."*
>
> *Proverbs 21:17*

In today's culture, it seems like the only thing people like to do is "have a good time." An entire movement exists in which people are committed to pursing pleasure as a matter of personal ethics—hedonism. But, this is almost the opposite of why we were created.

According to Revelation 4:11, we were created for God's pleasure, not for our own. We should be seeking to please Him, not ourselves. Actually, I consider it a test of someone's love for Christ—if you love Him, your pleasure *is* to please Him. That's not just a spiritual principle, either. Even in natural love, a person's desire is to please the one that they love. Why should not the same apply to our love for God?

Do you want to be wealthy so that you can do what you want when you want, or do you want to be wealthy so that you can have more resources with which to serve God? Sure, personal enjoyment is one of the purposes of wealth, but it should be the last consideration.

Lack Inducer #6: Impure Motives

> *"But the LORD said unto Samuel, Look not on his countenance, or on the height of his stature; because I have refused him: for the LORD seeth not as man seeth; for man looketh on the outward appearance, but the LORD looketh on the heart."*
>
> 1 Samuel 16:7

I cannot overstate how important motives are to everything we do. God is immeasurably concerned about the state of our hearts, and our reasons for doing what we do. Impure motives pull the rug out from under our efforts and practically guarantee failure.

Simply being a Christian does not qualify you to pursue wealth in a godly way. While you may have become a new creature through the salvation experience, your purposes for pursuing wealth must be aligned with that Christian ideal.

"A faithful man shall abound with blessings: but he that maketh haste to be rich shall not be innocent...[22] He that hasteth to be rich hath an evil eye, and considereth not that poverty shall come upon him."

Proverbs 28:20, 22

Who is "he that maketh haste to be rich?" The easiest example to point out is a gambler. Gamblers gamble because they want to be rich and they want it quickly. But, quick riches are not God's will for your life. There are lessons that must be learned on the journey to wealth, things that you probably won't understand if you don't build your wealth through hard work and wise decisions. That's why even the few people who do hit it big with the lottery wind up broke again a few years later.

Now, don't read this passage and conclude that God doesn't want you wealthy, or that He doesn't want you to make sound decisions with His promises of wealth in mind. The point made here is that your pursuit isn't supposed to be for wealth itself, but for the will of God. While the will of God for His people *is* wealth, His will must be our aim, not the wealth itself. In other words, wealth is the means, not the end.

"Wilt thou set thine eyes upon that which is not? for riches certainly make themselves wings; they fly away as an eagle toward heaven."

Proverbs 23:5

When I first ran across this passage, it made me laugh. I don't know if it was the imagery of money sprouting wings and flying off, or if it was the absolute truth of the statement itself. One thing I've learned in this life is that money comes and money goes. It makes a wonderful tool, but a horrible treasure. I don't recommend depending on it—and certainly not idolizing it—because it may be here today and gone tomorrow.

So, make sure that your motivations are right, because your financial situation may not be as sure and stable as you think—especially if God tells you to give it all away, as Jesus did to the young ruler who wanted to be His disciple (Luke 18:18-23).

If you're only reading this book so you can learn how to be rich, you're motivations are totally off. Your purposes and priorities for wealth should reflect God's purposes and priorities: 1) Kingdom advancement, 2) Benevolence, and 3) Personal Enjoyment. Notice that personal enjoyment is the least important of all three purposes, although still a valid part of the prosperity reality.

Lack Inducer #7: A Poverty Mentality

Poverty isn't just a financial state, but a state of mind. Actually, the poverty *mentality* is more insidious than the impoverished financial state because even if the financial state changes, it doesn't guarantee a change of mentality; and if the poverty mentality doesn't change, it will eventually reproduce the financial state in your life.

Your way of thinking is vitally important to what will manifest

117

in your life. Not only does your thinking determine who you are as a person, but it also has a lot to do with what you'll have and what you'll do with it.

"For as he thinketh in his heart, so is he…"
Proverbs 23:7a

"And be not conformed to this world: but be ye transformed
by the renewing of your mind, that ye may prove what is that
good, and acceptable, and perfect, will of God."
Romans 12:2

Get your thinking in line with God's word and you can't go wrong! Do it not, and even if riches come, they won't last. The choice is yours…

The Devil Called "Debt"

The big problem is that so many people, particularly in the middle class, have allowed our culture to put blinders on them so that they can't perceive what's right before their eyes—poverty isn't as far away as they may think. The road to poverty is much broader than many people realize.

But is poverty really such a bad thing? People have traditionally preached for years that poverty was godly. In fact, Catholic doctrine hails those who have taken a vow of poverty. Yet, despite these affirmations of poverty that have invaded the Church, we need to find out what God has to say about the state of being poor.

> *"The rich man's wealth is his strong city: the destruction of the poor is their poverty."*
>
> *Proverbs 10:15*

Notice that wealth is a strong city, a defense. Poverty, on the other hand, is a source of destruction. That revelation reminds me of the purpose of the thief in Jesus' teaching...

> *The thief cometh not, but for to steal, and to kill, and to destroy: I am come that they might have life, and that they might have it more abundantly.*
>
> *John 10:10*

One of the purposes of the thief, who we recognize is Satan, is to destroy. Well, according to Proverbs 10:15, one of the sources of destruction is poverty. So then, Satan uses poverty (among other things) to limit and/or destroy God's people. Let me reiterate this point...

Poverty is a weapon of the adversary, not a Christian virtue.

This scheme has worked long enough, child of God. It's time to get the word out that God has a better plan for His people.

As I was thinking about poverty, I began to see that it's very similar to hell. If we were to consider poverty a "place" instead of a financial "condition", the following comparisons could be made between it and Hell:

1. Both are among the most commonly talked about "places" in the Gospels.
2. The roads to both destinations are broad.
3. You don't have to work hard to get to either place.
4. Although most people don't want to be in either place, in most cases, lifestyles indicate indirect decisions to ensure a home there.
5. Most people who [will] find themselves in either place are shocked because they're in denial about the choices that led them there.
6. God doesn't want you in either place.
7. Two of the purposes Jesus came to accomplish were to deliver people from the power of both.

Before going on, let me define the term "poverty", because for the purposes of this book, it's important we have the same definitions in mind. According to the dictionary, impoverished simply means "poor enough to need help from others" or "in a state of financial insufficiency". After applying this definition to your own life, would you have to conclude that you're presently impoverished?

In American culture, private ownership is the "way of the world". Unfortunately, our capitalist way of life (which is generally a good thing, by the way) has taught people that ownership defines them. In response to that warped message, people are programmed to do three things: buy, buy, and buy… What we can't seem to realize, however, is that buying something does not necessarily make you the owner of it.

Think about how many cars people have that they actually don't own. And what about houses, the pinnacle of private ownership? Do you realize how many people are close to being homeless and don't realize it? If you have a mortgage, car loan, credit cards, and any other types of debt, the sad (and biblical) reality is that you aren't walking in God's best for you. Quite literally, you're in bondage.

To me, the fact that so many people "need" credit cards or lines of credit indicates that they're impoverished and don't realize it. If you don't have money in the bank for rainy days (and therefore don't need a credit card for so-called emergency purposes), you're not financially sufficient. Past due bills and all other forms of financial insufficiency surely don't indicate that you're living in the wealthy place. So, the first stumbling block to overcome is that we need to be honest about the state of our finances, and stop defining ourselves by how many things we possess (whether we actually own them or not).

We've accepted mortgages, car notes, and credit cards as three types of borrowing that are perfectly acceptable and normal. But, I take issue with that conclusion. Technically, you don't own **anything** that you're still paying off. Don't believe me? Stop paying your mortgage and see who *really* owns that house. Stop paying your car note and you'll realize that *somebody* can take your car away and you won't be able to prosecute them for theft.

Consider the following passage, which I think clearly shows God's perspective on borrowing:

"The rich ruleth over the poor, and the borrower is servant to the lender."

Proverbs 22:7

This is a very sobering passage, to say the least. Think about it. If you're in debt, you're working to make someone else rich. When you get a paycheck, you're not free to do with it as you please (or even as God pleases) because morally, that money belongs to your creditors. How can this be God's best for you?

The last I heard, Christians are supposed to be servants (slaves) of God, and of no one and nothing else. But, debt makes this ideal impossible.

The enemy has tricked so many Christians into believing that various types of debt are okay. In doing so, Satan has enslaved them to a world-system that the Bible says he's the god of (2Co. 4:4).

Here's the real deal. Financial debt is an enemy of the Christian. Jesus said that if He makes you free, you're free indeed (John 8:36), but that doesn't sit well with the implications of financial debt.

You're **not** free when you're in debt. If God tells you to go to Japan to minister for 6 months, that would be a practical impossibility for most Christians because they have bills to pay. They have to keep their jobs because that's where the money's coming from (and steady income is made a necessity because of debt). Under such circumstances, the source of the paycheck (the J-O-B) becomes the dictator rather than God.

There are so many implications associated with debt, and none of them are positive. The fact that so many Christians—even after seeing how insidious debt is in the life of the believer—still believe that certain kinds of debt are perfectly fine is testimony to the reality that we've been brainwashed into believing that debt is a normal and acceptable way of life. But, according to the Bible (which is supposed to be our final authority), it isn't.

> *"Owe no man any thing, but to love one another: for he that loveth another hath fulfilled the law."*
>
> *Romans 13:8*

When I first read this passage, I have to admit I was challenged. What I read and what I'd previously accepted as "normal" didn't gel together. In fact, I started looking for ways to twist the obvious statement this passage was making so that it didn't require of me what it appeared to be requiring.

But, I thank God for the Holy Spirit, who gently reminded me that God's word must never be challenged. It was one thing to make sure I had the right interpretation, but another thing altogether to simply refuse to believe that it said something that wasn't easy to swallow. Having been reminded of this, I didn't stop examining the passage. I simply changed my motives, and decided that whatever the conclusion, I would accept it as absolute truth.

After humbly considering the various interpretations of the

123

passage, including the interpretation held by the commentary in my study Bible, I was forced to disagree with the conclusions held by so many and reaffirm my initial interpretation (the one I was hoping to change).

Basically, there are only two possible interpretations of the Romans passage.

1. All debt is wrong, or
2. Debt isn't wrong, but having outstanding debt is.

According to the first interpretation, all debt is wrong. This interpretation speaks out against mortgages, car loans, credit cards, student loans, lines of credit... It speaks against **all** types of debt.

The second interpretation, on the other hand, does not speak against having debt; rather, it speaks against having debt and not paying it back. If you look in many modern English version of the Bible, you'll see the verse translated as something like, "Don't **continue** to owe anyone," which points to this second interpretation as the biblically correct one.

These two interpretations are very different, so it's important to clearly know what the proper one is. I can certainly understand how different people can see different points being made in the passage, but it's important to see the point God put in the passage, not the points we read out of it.

After considering the language of the text, as well as how it harmonizes with other passages that speak to the issue of borrowing, I could arrive at no other conclusion but that the first interpretation is the correct one. That's not an easy pill to swallow, but it's the truth nonetheless. Allow me to explain…

The passage says, "Owe no man any thing, but to love one another." The problem is in how we interpret the word "owe", which is the Greek word *opheilo*. Apparently, it can be interpreted to mean "being indebted to" in the broad sense, or "being past due in your indebtedness" in the specific sense. So, a simple word study doesn't really help much. The key to knowing the proper interpretation of the word "owe" is actually found in the second half of the statement.

We are to owe no man *anything* **except** love. Now, let's apply this truth to the various interpretations of "owe" and see which one harmonizes with the overall spirit of the Bible. Let's look at each interpretation in turn.

1. Have no debts whatsoever except the debt of love, OR
2. Have no debts that you aren't faithfully paying on except the debt of love.

Now, if you read these two interpretations in light of their implications on our duty to love one another, it makes absolutely no sense for interpretation #2 to be correct. If such were the case, this passage would be saying that the only debt we **don't** have to pay faithfully is the debt of love. Forgive my language, but any idiot would know that this couldn't be what the Bible is trying to teach us.

Apparently, what the Bible is saying is that we should have no debt in our lives whatsoever except for the debt that we can never repay in full—the debt of love. The debt of love is the only debt that we should be paying on at all, because it's the only debt that should exist in our lives. That way, we're enslaved only to love rather than to Union Memorial Bank & Trust.

Here's the reality... Any attempt to force an alternative interpretation on the text is an indication of unwillingness to let the word speak for itself—and believe me, I understand how hard it can be to accept this truth. But when God's word speaks, we **must** agree.

So, debt of any kind (except the debt of love that we owe to God and repay by offering it to others) is not in keeping with God's perfect will for our lives. It is a ploy of the enemy to keep us enslaved. He figures that since he is no longer master of our spirits, he can at least be master of our finances. DON'T LET IT HAPPEN. If it has already happened, DON'T LET IT STAY THAT WAY.

Get and stay out of debt so that your only master is the Lord. In so doing, you can tell that devil called debt to "go to hell!"

NOTE: Mortgages, while not ideal, are one exception to the general rule that most (if not all) debt is bad. The reason is that, unlike renting an apartment, mortgages allow equity to be established. This actually makes mortgages a means of improving the financial circumstance of debtors, not enslaving them as other forms of debt do. One must pay for housing whether equity is being gained or not, so at least with a mortgage, one is actually building his financial status over time.

How To *REALLY* Help The Poor

One of the most horrible things we've done in contemporary

society is glorify poverty. We've made people feel like it's perfectly alright to be and stay poor, and that they don't have to worry because the government will take care of them through welfare payments. Certainly, not every impoverished person feels this way; but with increasing social programs, we are making many people dependent on financial assistance. In so doing, we're crippling them by denying them the hope of ever rising above their present state. This doesn't apply to everyone, but it's yet a problem we must address as a society.

Like a drug, social services have addicted the poor, and in many cases, have resulted in an entitlement syndrome that affects a countless number of people. Let me tell you—whether you're black or white, male or female, rich or poor, **nobody owes you anything!**

I don't care if you were done wrong in the past. Get over it... Move on... Put the pieces of your life back together because nobody else will. Don't let a person or circumstance keep you in bondage. Love yourself enough to rise above the expectation that somebody else has to do for you what you should be doing for yourself.

Nobody owes you a monthly check because you had a baby without being able to take care of it financially. Nobody owes you money because you're on your third child in as many years and haven't worked a steady job in twice as long. Nobody owes you food stamps because you'd rather watch Maury Povich on television than go out and cut lawns, collect cans, or do a host of other things to produce some level of consistent income in your life.

It's time for us as a society to stop rewarding poverty-inducing choices and lifestyles. And just in case you're wondering, the Bible agrees completely, but we'll get to that in a moment.

> **NOTE:** I know the previous few paragraphs were a bit harsh, and I promise it's not my intention to sound heartless. But, my whole point is that we've sugarcoated people into eternal servitude to poverty. It's time that the **truth** makes us all free.

I would now like to look at some very practical ways we can help the poor. I'm not talking about paying their bills or giving them a paycheck every month, either. We've all heard the adage: "Give a man a fish and he will eat for a day. Teach him how to fish and he will eat for a lifetime." Well, we're going to look at ways to empower the impoverished so that they won't stay that way. This is how you help someone who's poor!

Key #1: Don't Vote With Your Wallet

Now, I don't want to get too political in this book, but let me implore you—we **must** stop voting people into office who use the plight of the poor to help them get elected, never actually doing anything about the long-term effects that their hand-me-out policies will have on the impoverished. Don't vote for someone simply because you like their fiscal (financial) policies, or because they promise to put money in your pocket.

The apostle Paul said that the love of money was the root of all sorts of evil (1Ti. 6:10), and he was right. For promises of lower taxes on the middle class, we've voted people in office who support the *theory* of evolution being taught to our youth, yet oppose any

128

reference to Christianity in the classroom. For promises of increased social services, we've voted people in office who support abortion yet oppose capital punishment—a penalty God supports, by the way.

I don't know how this works, but apparently, it's acceptable to keep convicted murders alive and kill innocent babies. Better for the citizens to pay for a multiple murderer to eat three-square-a-day, work out, and watch cable TV until he dies of natural causes than for a woman to have to carry an unwanted baby for nine months and then give it up for adoption. What a world...

> *"And that, knowing the time, that now it is high time to awake out of sleep: for now is our salvation nearer than when we believed."*
>
> *Romans 13:11*

Key #2: Stop Giving To Leeches

The absolute worst thing you can do in trying to help someone in need is to continue to give to a person who has already demonstrated an unwillingness to help themselves.

> *"For even when we were with you, this we commanded you, that if any would not work, neither should he eat."*
>
> *2 Thessalonians 3:10*

I'll tell you a secret. The passage you just read was NOT rhetorical. If a person doesn't want to get a job (and isn't interested in learning skills to prepare himself for one), let him starve. That's right... Let him starve. It's time for the Church to start kicking some people out of the soup line, literally. We've crippled people beyond repair by giving to them over and over again even though they **refuse** to do the slightest thing to improve their own situation. We should learn from this biblical admonition and start making certain individuals deal with the repercussions of the choices they've made. That's the only way some people will ever open their eyes and rise above their lethargy.

Now, I'm not saying you should turn people away just because you've helped them more than once; but once you recognize that they aren't interested in changing their situation, cut them off! Don't satiate their desire for an immediate and temporary fix to a problem that will recur in a few days. Don't perpetuate their dependence by always coming to their rescue.

If a person made a few foolish mistakes, but truly wants a better life, you shouldn't hesitate to extend yourself. But, keep in mind that God is not calling you to be naïve, either. Don't be a soft touch. I guarantee that once some people know you'll always bail them out, they'll **never** learn to make better decisions. You could wind up being the very factor that cripples for life the one you love.

The sad truth: Some people must hurt a while if they're ever to move forward. Unfortunately, those to whom this applies usually don't know this until it's too late. But, better for someone to rise to excellence through a painful past than for him/her to be breast-fed off of someone else's kindness for the rest of his/her life. This happens all the time with parents who keep bailing their grown

130

children out of trouble.

Here's a case in point—Abraham and Lot. In this story, Abraham just couldn't bear to leave his nephew at home like God told him to. He took Lot along with him and wound up having to always come to his rescue. Lot leeched off of Abraham's blessing—something God tried to prevent by telling Abraham to leave all of His kinfolk back in Haran.

Get rid of the "Lot" in your life.

Key #3: Give To Private Empowerment Organizations

Give financial contributions to private organizations that don't simply feed the poor, but that help the poor to rise above their impoverished status. Find organizations that teach the impoverished basic life and trade skills. These types of organizations need all the help they can get, especially the faith-based ones.

Key #4: Get To Know Those You Help

If you participate in some type of program where you can personally meet the recipients of the program's assistance (like a church's food pantry, clothing outreach, or other public assistance program), don't be content to simply give, give, give. Take a personal interest in these people's lives. See them as more than just a group of people you're trying to clear out of the help line. See them as individuals whom God created in His image—people He loves and wants so much better for.

It's so easy to get caught up in the *work* of benevolence without actually connecting with the people you're helping. But, that's a mistake. You'd be surprised how much the simple act of taking a personal interest in someone can motivate them to want to do better for themselves. Some people have lost their will to press forward because it seems that nobody cares about them anymore. Show them that they're wrong!

"For the LORD God is a sun and shield: the LORD will give grace and glory: no good thing will he withhold from them that walk uprightly."

Psalms 84:1

Section Three

God's Economic System

When I consider the perception many Christians have of God's covenant of wealth, it's no wonder they don't see His promises manifested more fully in the Church. So many are quick to believe the promises regarding wealth, but slow to actually activate those promises over their lives. Then, when thing don't turn out like expected, they tend to blame God, rather than the man in the mirror.

The Body of Christ must come to understand that although God has made promises regarding our finances, there is a system in place that must be worked if manifestation is to actually take place. If we don't understand this system—and understand it well—how can we use it to produce the fruit of wealth in our lives?

Until the word on financial prosperity is *richly* dwelling in your heart in "*all* wisdom" (Col. 3:16), you won't be able to move beyond barely scratching the surface when it comes to biblical manifestation. Knowing that you want nothing less than God's intended best for your finances, let's dive right in and examine exactly how God's economic system operates.

7

The Tri-Fold Nature of Giving

The first thing it's important that you understand regarding God's economic system is that there are multiple types of giving. Often, when we think about the act of giving, we lump everything into one proverbial basket and consider it all offerings. But, giving is encapsulated in multiple acts, not just offerings. Once you understand these various acts, the functions they serve, and the promises of God attached to each, you'll be able to make the system reach its full potential in your life.

Tithes

> *"And all the tithe of the land, whether of the seed of the land, or of the fruit of the tree, is the LORD's: it is holy unto the LORD. [31] And if a man will at all redeem aught of his tithes, he shall add thereto the fifth part thereof. [32] And concerning the tithe of the herd, or of the flock,*

even of whatsoever passeth under the rod, the tenth shall be
holy unto the LORD. [33] He shall not search whether it
be good or bad, neither shall he change it: and if he change it
at all, then both it and the change thereof shall be holy; it
shall not be redeemed."

Leviticus 27:30-33

For the uninitiated, the tithe is 10% of your income, which God has declared belongs to Him. When you receive increase from your efforts (Deut. 14:22), 10% of it belongs to God.

The first thing people think about when they see a passage about tithing quoted from the Old Testament is, *Hey, that doesn't apply to Christians because that was under the Law.* It's amazing that these same people don't mind using instruments in church, even though the only time you see instruments used in earthly acts of praise and worship is in the Old Testament.

Everything written after the Law was instituted in the book of Exodus is **not** invalid. You have to understand *why* something was commanded or condemned in order to ensure it's applied properly to the Christian Church. I'll show you the purpose for the tithe in a moment, which will make it clear that it's still a necessary part of the Christian Church. In the meantime, let's look at what this passage in Leviticus is telling us about the tithe.

First of all, the tithe is holy. I hate that some denominations have come to be called "Holiness" churches because it has skewed people's perception of what it means to be holy. Holiness is not a *type* of Christian belief. It's not refusing to wear makeup. It's not wearing long dresses. Holiness is the quality of being pure, sanctified (set apart), and meet (fitting) for God's use. Now, if we apply this definition to the tithe, it can simply be stated that the tithe is "pure, separated from all other purposes, and fitting for God's use." Good God! Did you get that? If not, read it until you do.

Now, if the tithe is set apart for God's use, that means it *belongs* to Him. The tithe "is the Lord's", just as verse 30 emphatically states. When the tithe is not given to God, it is the equivalent of stealing, because you're taking something that has been purified and set apart by the Divine and using it for your own use. Not only is that a slap in the face to God's authority, but it's also a form of sacrilege—exalting your own purposes above those of God, to the extent that you take something *holy* and use it in a manner it was not set apart for.

Having understood that the tithe does not belong to you, you must recognize that technically, tithing is **not** an act of giving…

What??? That's right. According to the Scriptures, tithing is not an act of giving; it's an act of *bringing.*

> *"Will a man rob God? Yet ye have robbed me. But ye say,*
> *Wherein have we robbed thee? In tithes and offerings. [9]*
> *Ye are cursed with a curse: for ye have robbed me, even this*
> *whole nation. [10] Bring ye all the tithes into the storehouse,*
> *that there may be meat in mine house, and prove me now*
> *herewith, saith the LORD of hosts, if I will not open you*
> *the windows of heaven, and pour you out a blessing, that*
> *there shall not be room enough to receive it."*
>
> *Malachi 3:8-10*

137

According to this passage, you *bring* the tithe into the house of God. You're not *giving* the tithe to the Church; you're simply bringing to the Church what belongs to God. Let's get technical with it:

Tithes are ***brought*** to the Church and ***paid*** to God through the agency of the Church.

Think about it for a moment… How can you *give* God what doesn't belong to you? All the more, how can you give Him what already belongs to Him?

I'm sure there's someone out there who has the attitude that he did the world a favor because he paid someone back his/her money. But if I loan you money, you're not doing me a favor by paying me back; and you're most certainly not *giving* me money. This selfsame principle applies to the tithe.

The tithe belongs to God and it is your responsibility to render to Him what is His. This is exactly why the failure to do so is considered stealing (robbing God). People don't like to think of themselves as having robbed God, but that's how He looks at it. Think of how many Christians have robbed God because they had overdue bills. Think of how many Christians have robbed God to pay their mortgage. How dare we tell God that our other financial obligations mean more to us than His own divine purposes?

Moving on from the implications of *not* tithing (because I hope you love God and are committed to doing what pleases Him), I'd like to deal with the great blessings promised to those who *do* tithe

138

faithfully.

> *"Bring ye all the tithes into the storehouse, that there may be meat in mine house, and prove me now herewith, saith the LORD of hosts, if I will not open you the windows of heaven, and pour you out a blessing, that there shall not be room enough to receive it. [11] And I will rebuke the devourer for your sakes, and he shall not destroy the fruits of your ground; neither shall your vine cast her fruit before the time in the field, saith the LORD of hosts. [12] And all nations shall call you blessed: for ye shall be a delightful land, saith the LORD of hosts."*
>
> *Malachi 3:10-12*

When you bring the tithe into the storehouse and present it to God, His promise to you is wonderful! He promises to open the windows of Heaven itself and pour you out a blessing so large that you won't even be able to contain it. Many people can't imagine such a blessing, but I'm telling you that God holds true to His promises.

Not only will Heaven awaken over your life, but God will also rebuke the devourer for the sake of the tither. But, what's the devourer? The devourer is anything that pops up in your life and eats away your "bread"—your money.

- Have you ever experienced times when every little bit of extra money you came across was somehow drained away, and you had no idea where it went?

- Have you ever had plans for your income tax refund—how you were going to go on vacation or plant a seed into someone's life—but no sooner than you cashed the check, something happened and you had to use the money for something else?

- Have you ever gotten a raise and then wound up having to repair the furnace?

- Have you ever come across some extra money and wound up having to fix your car?

Oh, that pesky devourer! Isn't it good news that God will rebuke the devourer for your sake? Isn't it exciting to know that He'll give you a blessing and then make sure that the devourer can't consume it? Isn't it wonderful to know that God wants you to be able to enjoy your reward, and to not have to pay bills with it?

Look at the next promise to the tither, given in verse 12. Keep in mind that Israel was the only righteous nation in the earth. They were the chosen people of God. So, the fact that the heathen nations would call them blessed means that the blessing would be so obvious, so visible that people who didn't even know God would still recognize that they were blessed!

When you tithe, God promises to bless you so obviously that even sinners will call you blessed. You'll be so blessed that people who don't even know God will still know that *something* is happening in your life. They won't be able to deny it because they'll be able to see it with their own eyes!

"For this Melchizedek, king of Salem, priest of the most high God, who met Abraham returning from the slaughter of the kings, and blessed him; [2] To whom also Abraham gave a tenth part of all; first being by interpretation King of righteousness, and after that also King of Salem, which is, King of peace; [3] Without father, without mother, without descent, having neither beginning of days, nor end of life; but made like unto the Son of God; abideth a priest continually. [4] Now consider how great this man was, unto whom even the patriarch Abraham gave the tenth of the spoils. [5] And verily they that are of the sons of Levi, who receive the office of the priesthood, have a commandment to take tithes of the people according to the law, that is, of their brethren, though they come out of the loins of Abraham: [6] But he whose descent is not counted from them received tithes of Abraham, and blessed him that had the promises. [7] And without all contradiction the less is blessed of the better. [8] And here men that die receive tithes; but there he receiveth them, of whom it is witnessed that he liveth. [9] And as I may so say, Levi also, who receiveth tithes, paid tithes in Abraham. [10] For he was yet in the loins of his father, when Melchizedek met him."

Hebrews 7:1-10

If you've been taught about the priesthood of Melchizedek, you know that he was a *type* of Christ in that he had no recorded parentage and no recorded birth or death. In the same way, the eternal Son, Jesus, had no divine parentage, and certainly no date of

141

divine birth or death. (We recognize that in His physical manifestation, He did, but in eternity, He has no beginning.) This passage teaches that in Christ, the priesthood changed from the order of Aaron (of the tribe of Levi) to the order of Melchizedek, an eternal priesthood.

Now, I don't want to go into a detailed teaching on the change in priesthood—although a wonderful subject indeed. Suffice it to say, Melchizedek was a type of Christ. In fact, many scholars believe that he actually *was* Christ, a Christophany (an appearance of the pre-incarnate Christ), although that is a disputed assertion.

The second verse of this passage states that the patriarch Abraham gave Melchizedek a tithe of all his spoils of war. For all of those who believe tithing was only practiced under the Law, this event took place 500 or so years before the Law was even instituted.

The interesting part is that Paul teaches in verse 9 that although Levi was still in the loins of Abraham—he was Abraham's future grandson—he spiritually paid tithes in Abraham through Abraham's act of tithing to Melchizedek.

What do we learn from this passage? When you tithe, your children and grandchildren (down to the fourth generation – Ex. 43:7) are spiritually tithing *through* you. So, when you tithe, you're setting your future generations up for the tither's blessing. What an inheritance to leave to your children!

These are the promises to faithful tithers. I challenge you to become one. Try Him and see if He won't do just what He said (Mal. 3:10b).

Is tithing required for New Testament Christians?

I previously stated that we would look at the *purpose* of the tithe in order to determine if tithing is still applicable to the New Testament Church. If the purpose of the tithe is still a necessity, we can conclude that the tithe is still a necessity. This purpose is clearly borne out in Malachi 3:10.

> *"Bring ye all the tithes into the storehouse, that there may be meat in mine house, and prove me now herewith, saith the LORD of hosts, if I will not open you the windows of heaven, and pour you out a blessing, that there shall not be room enough to receive it."*

According to this passage, the purpose of the tithe is to provide financial substance (meat) for the house of God. Ever since the worship of God was institutionalized, the places dedicated to that worship and service have been called the house of God, and those houses have needed resources by which to operate.

So, I ask you a question: Does God still have a house in the earth—and I'm not talking about our physical bodies, but a place consecrated for His worship and service? Absolutely! Although we wrongly state that the buildings are churches (for *we* are the church), God definitely still has houses of worship set up throughout the world, as indicated by 1Ti. 3:15. So then, the tithe is still God's plan to keep those houses operating.

Detractors are quick to point out that the only type of giving expressed in the New Testament is freewill giving, not compulsory giving. They claim that the local church should have all it needs met by freewill offerings, and that the tithe is not necessary. I have three responses to such claims:

1. Tithing is not *giving*, so it really doesn't apply to the *freewill* type of giving that should take place.
2. The New Testament Church should not tithe out of obligation or compulsion, but out love for God and a realization that the tithe is still applicable, necessary, and expected by God.
3. If all that is required for the Church to operate is freewill offerings, why would God have required the tithe even for Old Testament followers?

The tithe is God's established system for keeping the institution of the Church with the resources it needs to continue operating. Detractors—often motivated not out of a sincere desire for biblical truth, but out of a frustration with having to part with 10% of their income—may not want to acknowledge this reality, but it's a reality nonetheless.

Another claim people often make when trying to "get out of" tithing is that there is no mention of the tithe in the Church Age (from the day of Pentecost onward), and so it is obviously not required of the Christians who comprise the Church. But, I'd like to offer the following food for thought…

What people often fail to consider is that the near-absence of the tithe in the Church Age scriptures actually serves as affirmation of its continuation. Keep in mind that tithing was an integral part of Jewish custom. Because most early Christians were Jews, their practices, no doubt, carried over into the Church Age.

Consider the practice of circumcision. Because the Jews continued this ritual, and even began requiring Gentile converts to be circumcised, a council had to be held to determine the Church's official doctrine on the matter (Acts 15:1-29).

The fact that the apostles never once found it necessary to teach against the necessity of tithing—as they found it necessary to do with regard to physical circumcision—serves as a strong indication that the practice did, in fact, continue without dispute in the New Testament Church. Its practice was never a point of doctrinal contention, neither in the Church's historic account in Acts, nor in the apostolic epistles.

"And here men that die receive tithes; but there he receiveth them, of whom it is witnessed that he liveth."

Hebrews 7:8

In this passage, Paul made a vital statement regarding the New Testament practice of tithing. He asserted that although men that eventually die receive the tithe here on Earth, in Heaven, Jesus Himself receives the tithe. Now, this expresses a very important point, so follow me closely here...

The priestly order did not change from Aaron's order to the order of Melchizedek until we entered into the New Covenant (Heb. 7:12). In other words, Jesus did *not* serve as our high priest until *after*

145

His resurrection from the dead and subsequent ascension back to Heaven (Heb. 8:1).

So, in order for Jesus to receive (note the *present* tense) tithes, He, of necessity, would be receiving these tithes *after* the New Covenant was instituted; for prior to this time, He was not serving as high priest, and could not have received the tithe.

Take note that although it says in Heb. 6:20 that Christ is our high priest forever, it does *not* say that He is our *eternal* high priest. His priesthood did, in fact, have a starting date, although it will never end. It was only *after* the Old Covenant was disannulled (Heb. 7:18) and the priesthood changed from the order of Aaron to the order of Melchisedek, that Jesus was "*made* a high priest" (Heb. 6:20) after this new order.

Now, if Jesus became our high priest *after* the time of the Law, yet received tithes *as* high priest, that means that people were tithing *after* the time of the Law, while Jesus was (and is today) serving as high priest.

This proves without the shadow of a doubt that the New Testament Church did, in fact, tithe; for Jesus did not receive tithes from Old Testament saints because He was not serving as high priest during that era. Paul acknowledged in this tiny verse tucked away in the 19th book of the New Testament that the early Church did indeed tithe—contrary to what some Christians would have us believe.

Now, if Christ is receiving our tithes as high priest, a failure to tithe is a failure to recognize that the priesthood did, in fact, continue into the New Covenant. The only difference is that while human agency receives our tithes here on Earth, Christ, our high priest forever, receives them in Heaven.

If tithing is still practiced under this New Covenant, then the tithe is still holy unto the Lord. And if the tithe is still holy, those who do not tithe are still sinning, robbing God of what He has declared by divine decree belongs to Him. For those who want an excuse not to tithe, this may not be an easy pill to swallow, but it's the Bible truth nonetheless. The tithe is still holy, it must still be *brought* into the storehouse and paid to its rightful owner, and the failure to do so is still sin.

Offerings

While your tithe is what you *bring* to the storehouse to *pay* God what is already His, your offering is what you give to God above and beyond your tithe. Once your tithe has been paid (and you're "square with the house"), you're then in a position to actually offer God a gift.

It's important that you understand something at this point. If you have not paid your tithes, your offerings don't mean much. How can you give God something when you're still in debt to Him?

Let's look at this practically. If I loan you $150 and you don't pay me back when you're supposed to, it would seem really silly of you to call yourself *giving* me $20. I wouldn't consider that a gift. I'd just consider it $20 off of your debt. In the same way, when you haven't tithed, you're in debt to God, and anything you give is just knocking a bit off of your debt. But, in fact, you still have actually *given* Him nothing.

Let's take that a step further. If you pay your tithes and that's it, you've still *given* God nothing. There are many Christians who think they've done their "reasonable service" when they tithe, and so they don't give an offering. Usually, this is because they perceive the tithe as though it were simultaneously a tithe and an offering. But in reality, they have given God nothing if they haven't given **above** the tithe.

You'll notice in Malachi 3:8 (quoted in the tithing sub-section) that God wasn't just robbed when people didn't tithe. He was also robbed in offerings. So, it's not as though you're supposed to tithe, but it's okay if you don't give an offering. To the contrary, if you don't give a tithe *and* an offering, God feels robbed.

Years ago, I was on a church's finance committee. During that time, I came to see how many Christians think when it comes to tithes and offerings. There were some who never tithed, and there were some who faithfully tithed, but rarely gave an offering. Only a faithful few were consistent in both tithes and offerings, and I've always thought that was a shame.

One of the problems people have when it comes to their offering is that the amount of their offering is usually determined by how much money they have left after they've paid their bills, put gas in their car, filled their cupboard with food, and kept enough for spending money until the next pay period. In effect, offerings are usually a very low priority in people's lives. Many have heard enough teachings on tithing to take it off of the top, but even many of *those* people don't allow their offerings to have the same place of preeminence in their finances.

Let's examine how God feels when you don't make Him your

first priority when it comes to what you do with your money? (Keep in mind that I'm talking about the money that belongs to you, not your tithe, which belongs to God.)

> *"A son honoreth his father, and a servant his master: if*
> *then I be a father, where is mine honor? and if I be a*
> *master, where is my fear? saith the LORD of hosts unto*
> *you, O priests, that despise my name. And ye say, Wherein*
> *have we despised thy name? [7] Ye offer polluted bread upon*
> *mine altar; and ye say, Wherein have we polluted thee? In*
> *that ye say, The table of the LORD is contemptible. [8]*
> *And if ye offer the blind for sacrifice, is it not evil? and if ye*
> *offer the lame and sick, is it not evil? offer it now unto thy*
> *governor; will he be pleased with thee, or accept thy person?*
> *saith the LORD of hosts.*
>
> *Malachi 1:6-8*

When your offering isn't your top financial priority, or when you give grudgingly and not cheerfully, you're offering polluted "bread" (money) to God. With such an act, God is not pleased.

During Old Testament times, the Israelites would offer God substance from their agriculture (which was the economy of the day). They would offer the crops and herds as offerings to God. But, look at the kind of so-called gifts they were giving. According to verse 8, they were offering the worst of their flock—what they figured they could do without. They offered blind animals, lame and sick. God called that type of attitude toward Him evil.

Unfortunately, this is the very same thing many Christians do today. We give Him an offering of what we think we can do without. We give Him what's left over after we've paid our bills and filled our cupboards. How dare we make God anything less than our first consideration?

God is slow to anger (Joel 2:13), but these evil acts angered Him. He responded by saying, in effect, "Look, a son honors his father, and a servant honors his master, but where is my honor? Looking at the filth of your offerings, I surely don't see the so-called honor you claim to give me. I can't tell that you love me like you say you do." It sounds to me like polluted offerings actually hurt God's feelings. What a horrible thing we tell God when He isn't the first consideration.

Dealing with the bad types of offerings only takes us halfway there. Let's turn the proverbial page and talk about the types of offerings that God is well pleased to receive.

"And Araunah looked, and saw the king and his servants coming on toward him: and Araunah went out, and bowed himself before the king on his face upon the ground. [21] And Araunah said, Wherefore is my lord the king come to his servant? And David said, To buy the threshingfloor of thee, to build an altar unto the LORD, that the plague may be stayed from the people. [22] And Araunah said unto David, Let my lord the king take and offer up what seemeth good unto him: behold, here be oxen for burnt sacrifice, and threshing instruments and other instruments of the oxen for

wood. [23] All these things did Araunah, as a king, give

unto the king. And Araunah said unto the king, The

LORD thy God accept thee. [24] And the king said unto

Araunah, Nay; but I will surely buy it of thee at a price:

neither will I offer burnt offerings unto the LORD my God

of that which doth cost me nothing. So David bought the

threshingfloor and the oxen for fifty shekels of silver. [25]

And David built there an altar unto the LORD, and

offered burnt offerings and peace offerings. So the LORD

was entreated for the land, and the plague was stayed from

Israel."

2 Samuel 24:20-25

Every time I read this, it speaks to me on a very personal level because when it comes to giving, it's important that I always remind myself of the principle conveyed here. In this passage, David purchased the threshing floor in order to build an altar to the Lord on the site.

Now, what's presently applicable is the exchange between David and Araunah. David expressed His intention to purchase the threshing floor; but because Araunah couldn't imagine selling something to the king, he tried to simply *give* the plot of land to David. Now, a typical person would accept the gift and say, "Thank you." A typical person, but not David.

David's response shows us exactly why God hailed him as a man after His own heart (1 Sam. 13:14). In contemporary language, he replied, "No. I've got to buy it from you. I can't offer God something that didn't cost me anything."

David understood a wonderful prosperity principle. What you offer to God **must** cost you something. If your offering doesn't cost you anything, wherein lies the meaning? If you have a thousand dollars in the bank, and give God $5, how can you reason that He'll be well pleased to receive that offering from you?

Think about David's example the next time you're writing out your offering envelope and ask yourself, *Is this amount really costing me anything? What am I saying to God by giving this amount?*

Keep in mind how God felt about the worthless offerings the people were giving in Mal. 1:6-8. Don't be like those people, who only gave God something they could do without, something that wasn't substantial and wouldn't be missed.

If your offering isn't meaningful to you, it will not be meaningful to God.

When was the last time your offering challenged you? In fact, do you even remember how much you gave in the offering this past Sunday? Unless you give the same amount each week, you probably don't remember. But, when your offering is substantial, you don't forget it. When your offering moves you, nobody has to remind you what the amount was. I challenge you to challenge yourself in your giving. Make your offerings substantial. Demonstrate God's worth in your giving—or at least try to (there really isn't enough money in the world to fully demonstrate His worth).

When I talk about giving a substantial seed, I'm not talking about a specific amount. To some, $500 is a drop in the bucket, but to others, it's a week's wage and would be a pretty substantial seed. So, only you know what's substantial to you; and don't forget, God knows, too.

> *"And Jesus sat over against the treasury, and beheld how the people cast money into the treasury: and many that were rich cast in much. [42] And there came a certain poor widow, and she threw in two mites, which make a farthing. [43] And he called unto him his disciples, and saith unto them, Verily I say unto you, That this poor widow hath cast more in, than all they which have cast into the treasury: [44] For all they did cast in of their abundance; but she of her want did cast in all that she had, even all her living."*
>
> *Mark 12:41-44*

Watch this—Jesus sat next to the offering plate and watched how much money people were giving in the offering. Talk about politically incorrect – I love it! Today, people would convulse with rage if someone took an interest in the *amount* of their giving. They'd immediately respond, "Hey, that's between me and God!"

But apparently, God is concerned about the *amount* of your offering, in addition to the spirit it's given in. Now, He doesn't care about the figure itself, but how much is given in relation to a person's overall financial worth. When Jesus saw the poor widow cast in an amount that was **very** small yet **very** substantial to her (it was her entire "income"), He was impressed. As far as He was concerned, she'd given more than anyone else.

Let me ask you a question: When was the last time you gave God your entire paycheck, as this poor widow did? Let me ask you *this* question: Is God even *worth* your entire paycheck? I'll give you the benefit of the doubt here and assume you answered, "Yes." That being the case, why haven't you ever given your entire paycheck (if your answer to the first question was in the negative)? Most likely, it's because you have bills to pay. But, that's exactly the point of this whole section. If you gave your entire paycheck because you didn't have anything else to do with it, it would no longer be a substantial seed, and you'd be in the same boat as the rich people who gave much more than the poor widow, even though they gave less. (Did you catch that?)

Child of God, you honor the Lord when you give a gift it hurts to give. I'm not saying to give every paycheck from now until the Rapture. But, I *am* saying that it's important that you demonstrate sacrificial giving from time to time, even if only to remind yourself in a meaningful way how much God really means to you.

Are you thinking, *Pastor, I hear what you're saying, but let's be real. That'll never happen.* If so, I first applaud you for your honesty. But, immediately after the short applause, I've got to tell you—this is the reason it's so difficult to activate the prosperity anointing in the believer's life. You've got to cultivate the prosperity mentality, otherwise you'll never be able to exercise the level of faith required to make your offerings meaningful.

Firstfruits

The firstfruits is about the most misunderstood of all the types of giving. Most people equate it with the tithe when, in fact, the two are totally different. I can't say that I don't know why the firstfruits has been so misunderstood. It's not as though the Bible makes the issue plain and clear, as it does with the tithe and the offering.

"Honor the LORD with thy substance, and with the firstfruits of all thine increase: [10] So shall thy barns be filled with plenty, and thy presses shall burst out with new wine."

Proverbs 3:9-10

In Malachi 1:6-8, we saw how God feels when He's not our top financial priority. The actual word He uses is *honor*, saying, "If I am a father, where is my honor?" Now, the passage in Malachi was actually referring to the offerings of the people; however, this passage in Proverbs shows that we not only honor God with our offerings, but also with our firstfruits.

Oftentimes, tithes and firstfruits are considered the same thing. You've probably heard the two terms used interchangeably. However, it's important to understand that they are two different types of giving, as clearly indicated by the following passage:

"And at that time were some appointed over the chambers
for the treasures, for the offerings, for the firstfruits, and for
the tithes, to gather into them out of the fields of the cities the
portions of the law for the priests and Levites: for Judah
rejoiced for the priests and for the Levites that waited."

Nehemiah 12:44

You'll notice in this passage that the offerings, firstfruits, and tithes are mentioned in turn, indicating that they are distinct methods of giving, and that all three are to be brought to the Lord. Clearly then, the tithe and the firstfruits are not the same thing.

But, what exactly is the firstfruits? How does it differ from the general freewill offering and the tithe?

"And to bring the firstfruits of our ground, and the
firstfruits of all fruit of all trees, year by year, unto the house
of the LORD…"

Nehemiah 10:35

The firstfruits are the first annual harvest of the ground, which is representative of everything that comes afterward. It's the first produce taken up for that year. Giving it to God is an expression of gratitude and an acknowledgement that He is the true source of all increase.

The firstfruits are given on an annual basis, as shown by this passage in Nehemiah. It's the first of the receipts, which in the days of ancient Israel would have been all that was taken up on the first day of harvest. Translating this into today's economy, the firstfruits are the first day's wages of each year. Because of our economic system, it would also encompass the first of any additional income-producing activities engaged in after the initial firstfruits was given in that year.

Oh my God! How can I give an entire day's wages, especially so soon after Christmas? Well first, I can tell you that you don't have to *give* your first day's income. To the contrary, you're supposed to **bring** your firstfruits, just as with the tithe.

The difference between the firstfruits and the tithe is that the tithe is holy by its very nature, while the firstfruits must be *made* holy by being offered to God as a representation of all the income that follows for the remainder of the year. Notice that in Romans 11:16, the apostle Paul says that *if* the firstfruit be holy, the lump is holy. "If" indicates that it's not a foregone conclusion that the firstfruit is holy. To the contrary, it is *made* holy when given to the Lord. Only then is the "lump" (the income that follows) also made holy.

Not only is the firstfruit supposed to be given at the first of the year for all existing streams of income (jobs, investments, etc.), it's also supposed to be given on any new income-producing ventures that you become engaged in throughout the year. So, if you invest in the stock market in April, the first day's worth of income you receive should go to God as the firstfruits, and then the first day's dividend of each year should go to Him as the normal yearly firstfruits.

You can see the principle of the firstfruits in action when you read the story of the fall of Jericho. This city-state was the first Canaanite land to be conquered by the Israelites. As the first, its spoils were holy unto the Lord.

"And it came to pass at the seventh time, when the priests blew with the trumpets, Joshua said unto the people, Shout; for the LORD hath given you the city. [17] And the city shall be accursed, even it, and all that are therein, to the LORD: only Rahab the harlot shall live, she and all that are with her in the house, because she hid the messengers that we sent. [18] And ye, in any wise keep yourselves from the accursed thing, lest ye make yourselves accursed, when ye take of the accursed thing, and make the camp of Israel a curse, and trouble it. [19] But all the silver, and gold, and vessels of brass and iron, are consecrated unto the LORD: they shall come into the treasury of the LORD."

Joshua 6:16-19

Joshua understood the principle of the firstfruits well. He made sure the Israelites understood that the spoils from this first conquest were to be put into the treasury of the Lord. He called the spoils "accursed things" because they belonged to God and would produce a curse if defiled. Unfortunately, Achan, didn't get the memo.

Achan took some of the spoils of war for himself and hid them in the ground beneath his tent. As a result of this defiling of the firstfruits, Israel lost its next battle, which was against the city-state of Ai. After Joshua laid before the Lord, asking why He allowed them to be defeated, God told him that they had a thief in their midst who had cursed the whole nation by taking of the "accursed things".

After Achan was identified as the thief, he, his family, all his belongings, and even the defiled spoils that he stole were taken away.

158

They (Achan, his family, and even his cattle) were all stoned and then everything (including the dead bodies) was burned with fire. This act of attrition caused God to relent of His anger, and Ai fell to the Israelites. (Joshua 7-8)

The moral of the story: The firstfruits belong to God. When you pay the firstfruits to God, you honor Him, as was explicitly stated in Proverbs 3:9.

As Christians, we should not give out of fear. However, we are to give as an act of obedience, gratitude, and recognition of the fact that all we have is only possible because of the Lord's goodness.

Where should the firstfruits be given? Unlike tithes and offerings, which are brought to the storehouse (the local church, Mal. 3:10), the firstfruits are to be given to the priest (or the modern day equivalent, the pastor—the head of the spiritual house). As a result, the blessing will rest in your house.

> *"And the first of all the firstfruits of all things, and every*
> *oblation of all, of every sort of your oblations, shall be the*
> *priest's: ye shall also give unto the priest the first of your*
> *dough, that he may cause the blessing to rest in thine house."*
> *Ezekiel 44:30*

God's Perspective On Your Giving
In your tithes and firstfruits, He sees your obedience.
In your offerings, He sees your gratitude.

Other...

Tithes, offerings, and firstfruits actually aren't the only types of giving. They are, however, the methods of giving *to God*, and that's why this section is called "The Tri-Fold Nature of Giving". But, the Bible actually teaches about another type of giving: alms.

> *"...Blessed is he that considereth the poor: the LORD will deliver him in time of trouble."*
>
> *Psalm 41:1*

Alms are gifts given to the poor, and it is certainly a practice that God smiles upon. It is not given a lot of detail in this chapter because the purpose of this book is to focus on God's economy, which, as it applies to giving, deals primarily with methods of giving to Him in particular (through the agency of the Church).

That being said, I wanted to make sure to mention almsgiving because again, God is well pleased when you consider the poor.

> *"That I may cause those that love me to inherit substance; and I will fill their treasures."*
>
> *Proverbs 8:21*

8

The Law of Seedtime and Harvest

When we think about God's way of doing things, we tend to spiritualize everything. We often make the mistake of not realizing that although God is a spirit, He often interacts with us through the natural realm. For example, when He has a message to get to the Church, He doesn't usually do it through a booming voice from the sky, but rather through the mouth of a prophet.

When it comes to financial prosperity, God is no different. Since very early on, He's had a natural system in place to govern all matters of increase, including financial.

> *"While the earth remaineth, seedtime and harvest, and cold and heat, and summer and winter, and day and night shall not cease."*
>
> *Genesis 8:22*

This passage shows us God's response to the offering Noah gave after the floodwaters receded. His promise is that as long as the earth remains, four laws will always be in place:

- The law of seedtime and harvest
- The law of cold and heat
- The law of summer and winter
- The law of day and night

I want to focus on the first of these laws, and how it applies to the issue of financial prosperity. Seedtime and harvest is a law that governs the concept of sowing and reaping, a concept that farmers know and understand very well. They recognize that if you want to be able to take up crops in autumn, you have to have planted something months earlier.

> *"And he [Jesus] said, So is the kingdom of God, as if a man should cast seed into the ground; [27] And should sleep, and rise night and day, and the seed should spring and grow up, he knoweth not how. [28] For the earth bringeth forth fruit of herself; first the blade, then the ear, after that the full corn in the ear. [29] But when the fruit is brought forth, immediately he putteth in the sickle, because the harvest is come."*
>
> *Mark 4:26-29*

According to Jesus, the law of sowing and reaping (also

known as seedtime and harvest) is a picture of how the kingdom of God operates. So, this isn't just a nice cliché circling around the prosperity camp. It is God's economic system.

Seedtime and harvest is a law that mandates patience and faith in the life of the farmer. When he plants seeds into the ground, he cannot simply come back the next day and expect to take up his new crops. It takes time—an entire season even—for crops to grow and ripen for the harvest. This requires patience, because if the farmer doesn't wait until the crop is ready to be harvested, he can damage it, wasting all the time he spent in the fields.

Not only does this law exercise patience, but it also exercises faith. A farmer cannot simply plant a seed and return in four months expecting a fruitful crop. A good farmer that expects a healthy crop must tend to the crop from time to time, even when he doesn't see any results. It may take time for the sprout to break the ground as it grows, but that doesn't mean that the farmer stops tending the crop. So, whether he sees results or not, he's still tending to it because of the expectation of a harvest.

It's only when the crop has matured that it can be properly harvested; and it's when the crop is harvested that the farmer gets the benefit of the sowing he did months earlier.

So, seedtime and harvest is obviously a system that governs farming. Only when one sows can he reap. Only with patience and faith can he endure to the time of the harvest. But, these principles aren't limited to farming. Seedtime and harvest also applies to the kingdom of God, particularly to God's economic system.

"But this I say, He which soweth sparingly shall reap also sparingly; and he which soweth bountifully shall reap also bountifully. [7] Every man according as he purposeth in his heart, so let him give; not grudgingly, or of necessity: for God loveth a cheerful giver. [8] And God is able to make all grace abound toward you; that ye, always having all sufficiency in all things, may abound to every good work..."

2 Corinthians 9:6-9

Paul shows here that seedtime and harvest (sowing and reaping) isn't just a farming principle. It applies to finances, as well. He teaches that you will reap in the measure in which you sow. If you sow little, you'll reap little. If you sow a lot, you'll reap a lot. Seedtime and harvest governs giving and receiving; and therefore, it is vital to understand if you want to walk in financial prosperity.

When it comes to finances, people are generally interested only in reaping. They want more money, plain and simple. The Christian, however, needs to understand that because God's economy is governed by seedtime and harvest, you can't divorce receiving from giving. In fact, the latter is made possible by the former. You can't reap unless you have first planted; and even then, you have to have planted with the proper motivations.

It's important to understand the importance of this law. You can pray and fast, you can quote Scriptures and sing songs, but God's economic system is still what it is. Harvest is only given to those who sow seeds, and according to Genesis 8:22, this is the way it will be as long as the earth remains.

A short while ago, we looked at Mark 4:26-29, where Jesus likened the kingdom of God to sowing and reaping. Just in case you don't think this applies to finances, let's look at the preceding verses of the same text.

> *"And he said unto them, Take heed what ye hear: with what measure ye mete [give], it shall be measured to you: and unto you that hear shall more be given. [25] For he that hath, to him shall be given: and he that hath not, from him shall be taken even that which he hath."*
>
> *Mark 4:24-25*

So, the greater context of Mark 4:24-29 clearly establishes that Jesus is talking about giving. When one has dealt faithfully in their giving, they shall be given more. On the other hand, when someone has been stingy and as a result, hasn't harvested anything, what little he has will be taken away.

Before we move on, take a look at something Jesus said in this passage that I think is pretty profound. At the end of verse 24, He said that more will be given to those who hear. But to those that hear what? From the context, He's apparently talking about those who hear this particular message, which is clearly a message about giving and receiving, seedtime and harvest—the heart of the financial prosperity message.

So, when you hear and receive this word on financial prosperity, even more is put into your hands than if you just did the right thing but without a full understanding. In other words, a giver who simply gives because He loves God is promised a harvest. That's the law. However, a giver who gives because He loves God **and** because He understands the principles surrounding financial prosperity (because he's been taught it) will be given even more!

Now, if you compare this fact to the first thing Jesus said in verse 24, you arrive at a wonderful conclusion. He instructed us to "take heed to what [we] hear." Apparently, the Lord *wants* us to have more, and He understands that the way to having more is to hear the word on financial prosperity.

But, why should hearing the word on financial prosperity affect the measure of our harvest if we're giving the same amount as others who haven't heard the message? This is actually a very valid question considering that the harvest is directly connected to the amount sown. But, there's a very good answer.

Our motivation in giving should be love, in an effort to please God as faithful stewards. But, Hebrews 11:6 adds that it's impossible to please God without faith. So, how do you get faith? According to Romans 10:17, faith comes by hearing the word of God.

All you have to do is connect the dots. You must hear the word of God on financial prosperity and take heed to it (as Jesus instructed in Mark 4:24). Hearing this word produces faith, and taking heed to it produces the associated works, without which your faith would be dead (Jas. 2:26). Then, because you are exercising faith in your giving, your giving is well pleasing to God. Because your giving is well pleasing to God, He puts a supernatural unction **on top of the law of seedtime and harvest**, allowing you to reap in even greater measure than the law itself would have produced for you—and it's all because you heard the word on financial prosperity! Do you see how it works?

Your harvest is limited by the measure of your seed, and by the measure of your faith.

This makes Satan's plot to keep the financial prosperity message out of the pulpit even more insidious. He's trying to keep the believers broke so that He can keep the Church impotent to bring Kingdom explosion throughout the world (which any realistic person would agree costs money, and lots of it).

What's even worse is the fact that so many Christians are allowing Satan to manipulate them into contributing to his scheme's success. Anti-prosperity fanatics help to propagate the doctrine of devils, the intent of which is to limit the reach of the Kingdom in the earth by telling God's people that He's not interested in their financial status. Well, Mark 4:24-29 clearly puts that lie to rest.

> *"They that sow in tears shall reap in joy. [6] He that goeth forth and weepeth, bearing precious seed, shall doubtless come again with rejoicing, bringing his sheaves with him."*
> *Psalm 126:5-6*

Have you ever sown in tears? Have you ever given an amount that it really challenged you to give? Have you ever wrote out a check and thought to yourself, *God, what am I doing?* I sure have. In those moments, let this passage speak great comfort, and great anticipation for the harvest to come.

Those who have sown in tears shall reap in joy. Even when you have second thoughts about the amount of your seed, sow it anyway. You may go forth challenged, but you'll "**doubtless**" come again rejoicing, bringing in your harvest. Why? —Because you bore *precious* seed. You need to plant a seed that challenges you, that has you sowing "in tears" (metaphorically). This is the kind of sowing that gets God's attention.

I'm giving, you may think, *but I don't see how I'm going to make it to my next paycheck. I'm giving, but God, You're going to have to make a way out of no way. I'm going to give until it hurts, but I yet trust you for the harvest!*

Harvest is guaranteed when precious is your seed.

Understanding God's Proportions

According to the law of seedtime and harvest, you will receive a harvest when you sow, but the measure of your harvest will be in proportion to the seed you sow. But, what exactly does this mean? Will God return $100 if you give $100? How will you get increase if you're getting back in the same measure?

First, you have to understand that there's a big difference between a measure and an amount. Scripture never said that God would return your gifts in the *amount* given, but in the *measure*. You'll receive increase in the measure given, but in a greater amount. Now, if you're anything like me, you're probably wondering, *How is that possible. That doesn't make sense to me.*

To get a perspective on this seemingly contradictory usage of terms, let's examine a passage that clearly shows the distinction between a measure and an amount.

> *"Give, and it shall be given unto you, good measure, pressed down, and shaken together, and running over, shall men give into your bosom. For with the same measure that ye mete withal it shall be measured to you again."*
>
> *Luke 6:38*

In this single verse, two statements are made about the measure of your harvest that seem to contradict one another. First, Jesus says that you'll receive back *good* measure, pressed down, shaken together, and running over.

Now, have you ever taken out the trash when the bag was full and difficult to close? If so, you've probably done like I have and pressed the trash down and shaken it together in order to get rid of the air pockets so that the trash could be compacted together. Doing this usually makes more room in the bag so you can close it up.

Apply this trash bag analogy to Jesus' statement regarding the measure of your harvest. He says that even after you press it down and shake it together, it'll still be running over. That sounds like good measure, indeed.

But, how does that coincide with the statement that followed—that your harvest would be in the same measure with which you gave? It would seem that you'd either receive a "running over" harvest, or the same measure you initially gave. How can both be true?

When the Bible uses the term "measure" in this text, it is not referring to an amount, but to a portion or proportion. In other words, what Jesus was saying was that if you give in hundreds, you'll receive in hundreds. Now, the promise is that you'll receive more than you give, but that you'll still receive back in the general measure given. If your offering is in thousands, you'll receive a harvest in thousands. The harvested amount will be greater than the seed sown, but it will still be in the general measure of thousands.

The moral of the passage: The measure of your seed determines the measure of your harvest. As 2Co. 9:6 states, if you sow sparingly—although you'll reap in greater *amount*—you will reap in small measure (sparingly). Similarly, if you sow bountifully, you'll reap a greater amount, but in a bountiful measure.

This revelation exposes an important truth regarding the law of seedtime and harvest:

A great need requires a great seed.

If you have a large financial need that you're praying and believing God for, you have to activate His economic system in addition to praying. You must sow in order to reap. You must give in order to receive. But, remember that your harvest will be in the same measure that you give in. So, if your need is in the thousands, you'd be smart to plant a seed in the thousands. You can't give $5 and expect a $25,000 harvest just because you said, "Hallelujah!" God's economy, as we've seen, returns a greater amount (good measure,

170

pressed down, and shaken together) of the *measure* you give.

Consider that Mark 4:24 states the same principle—you'll reap in the same measure in which you sow. Why do you think He'd emphasize over and over again that your harvest would be in the same measure as your seed? Apparently, He wanted you to know exactly how His economy works so that you can tap into its power and activate it over your finances. There's no other logical explanation. Although you may know He wants to bless you with abundance, the only way He can do it is if you have an understanding of how prosperity operates. Why? –Because it's the law, established by God's own word, and He can't go against it. (Num. 23:19)

> *"Be not deceived; God is not mocked: for whatsoever a man*
> *soweth, that shall he also reap."*
>
> *Galatians 6:7*

This passage gives us very strong language. In fact, it underscores the unchangeable nature of the truth of sowing and reaping (seedtime and harvest) by staking God's honor on it—"God is not mocked". It's obvious that God's economy is not a group of nice suggestions but a real, operable, and efficacious system for producing abundance in the lives of believers. The thought that Christians would fight against this message when God is so obviously behind it really baffles me.

The Source of Increase

The world is a big place. If you're searching for a buried treasure, you need a map. A map will point you in the right direction and allow you to get where you need to be in order to find what you're looking for. When it comes to financial prosperity, God, through His word, has given us a map. He tells us exactly where to find increase, but we have to follow the map.

Let's look at the map and find out exactly what the source of financial increase is.

> *"Now he that ministereth seed to the sower both minister*
> *bread for your food, and multiply your seed sown, and*
> *increase the fruits of your righteousness"*
> *2Corinthians 9:10*

Here, Paul pronounces a blessing upon givers. If you're unsure that he's referring to givers, just read the greater context, beginning around verse 6.

At any rate, this blessing points out a principle that it's vital you understand if you're going to walk in financial prosperity. This principle is the key to God's economic system, so pay attention...

According to this passage, God ministers (or gives) seed to the sower. Now, the context makes it absolutely clear that seed refers to money and that the sowers are cheerful givers. So, what Paul's statement reveals is that God gives money to those who are cheerful givers of it.

Not only will He give seed (money) to the sower (giver), but

172

He'll also give bread for food. Now, what's bread in this context? Because bread is not mentioned in the context itself, we can only answer this question by considering the implications of the point Paul is making here. Apparently, both seed and bread refer to money. Seed refers to money that should be planted (given to ministry), and bread refers to money that can be consumed for personal wants and needs.

Here's another great principle (and a slight tongue twister): Not only will God give givers gifts to give, but He'll also give givers grain to gobble.

You **don't** want to consume your seed because the seed is your source of increase. It's only after you sow the seed that you reap the harvest. So, the last thing you want to do is take money God gave you for seed and consume it by paying bills or doing anything other than giving to ministry with it.

The key is to know how much of your money is seed and how much is bread. There's no formula involved in answering this issue. You simply must pray and be open to let God lead you in each individual instance of giving.

When you're filling out your offering envelope, ask God how much He desires for you to give. When you're planting a seed into a ministry (or into the life of a minister), ask Him what your seed amount is, because only He knows what He gave you for seed and what He gave you for bread.

Now, if you're going to ask God how much of your money is seed, you have to be content to follow His direction when He answers. If He gives you a figure that's much more than you originally intended to give, don't make the mistake of following your own opinion above God's direction (Prov. 3:5). Show Him that He can trust you to be a sower of seed.

Don't let your financial obligations manipulate you into consuming your seed. Seed must **always** be planted. You don't want to consume your source of increase. Seed may temporarily satisfy a pressing need, but if you would just plant it instead of consuming it, you can set yourself up for a lifetime of harvest.

But, understand this fact—Satan will make sure you have plenty of other pressing obligations that your seed can be used to meet. He'll swamp you with bills or other financial obligations in order to get you to cancel your own harvest. Don't fall for it! Always plant your seed, and you can trust that God will also give you bread for your needs.

Notice also in this verse that God will multiply your seed sown. If you don't sow the seed that He blesses you with, you leave Him nothing to multiply. Notice in Gen. 1:28 that before God told Adam and Eve to multiply, He told them to be fruitful. Before you can multiply, you must sow seed.

This is exactly what God is telling you to do in order to produce His brand of prosperity in your life—be fruitful (sow seed). When you sow seed, not only will He give you more seed to sow, but He'll also multiply the seed you've sown so that it produces an even greater harvest!

"There is that scattereth, and yet increaseth; and there is
that withholdeth more than is meet, but it tendeth to poverty.
[25] The liberal soul shall be made fat: and he that

watereth shall be watered also himself."

Proverbs 11:24-25

This passage emphasizes a very important prosperity principle: Don't let natural reason move you when it comes to your giving. According to this verse, there are some who give and yet increase more and more, and then there are those who won't give and are given to poverty. That doesn't make sense to the carnal mind; but in God's economy, it makes perfect sense because when you give, you open yourself up to receive.

You must release in order to increase.

The 25th verse promises that the giver ("the liberal soul") shall have plenty ("be made fat"), and the one who waters shall himself be watered. This is just another emphasis on the importance of being a seed-sower.

> *"And God said, Behold, I have given you every herb bearing seed, which is upon the face of all the earth, and every tree, in the which is the fruit of a tree yielding seed; to you it shall be for meat."*
>
> *Genesis 1:29*

In this passage, God is talking to Adam. What's amazing is that the source of increase and God's plan for provision was laid out right here in the first chapter of the Bible. When God provided what

Adam needed, He didn't do it by sending manna from Heaven every time Adam ate all that he had. He gave Adam the tool he needed to produce a constant flow of provision—a seed.

Everything God gave Adam to eat was something that bore seed. He empowered Adam to produce his own increase by giving him seed to sow. Now, if Adam decided he was too hungry, he could have chosen not to plant the seeds. He could have chosen simply to eat the seeds. But thankfully, he was smart enough to plant the seed and not consume it. Be Adam today. Be a sower of the seed and God will let the seed meet your need.

The Seed Form

I'm about to reveal something that will change your life if you grab hold and don't let go. Many Christians have prayed for something only to find that it didn't manifest in their lives. They incorrectly concluded that God didn't answer their prayer. But, the fact is that God always answers prayer, although He doesn't always give you what you asked for directly. Often, He answers your prayer by giving you the tool you need to produce the thing you prayed for yourself.

God has a way of answering your prayer by giving it to you in seed form. Instead of giving you the new car you prayed for, God may have given you a few hundred dollars. Now obviously, a few hundred dollars isn't a new car, but that doesn't mean that God didn't answer your prayer. What God did was give you *seed* to sow so that the seed sown would produce the bread you requested (the car). But, if you consume the seed because you don't recognize it as the answer to your prayer, you're actually consuming the very thing that will bring about your manifestation.

Don't consume your blessing just because it's in seed form. Your new house may be in seed form. Four thousand dollars can't buy a new house (under normal circumstances). Maybe God gave you that money so that you can plant a seed into the Kingdom, and in turn, He would give you more seed to sow **and** give you bread for food (money to purchase the house you prayed for).

Oh my God! Do you realize that when you consume your seed, you're actually trading your provision for a temporary fix? If you can just walk by faith and not by sight, you can begin to see a level of manifestation that you've never seen before. Let God increase you *His* way. Put His economic system to work and be a seed-sower—a giver. Don't consume your seed, because it just may be the answer to your prayer!

The Divine Partnership

What many Christians have yet to realize when it comes to financial prosperity is that wealth isn't just about you having plenty. It's literally a partnership between you and God for the purpose of advancing His Kingdom in the earth.

God gives seed to the sower because His ultimate purpose is for the seed to be sown into the Kingdom. If He can trust you to be a giver, a sower of seed, He'll give you more seed to sow. In effect, what God is looking for is an army of distribution centers—people through whom He can fund ministry. The great thing about God is that in addition to giving you more seed to sow, He'll also give you bread for your own enjoyment.

But, you can't just give once or twice and expect for God to trust you as a faithful distribution center. He's not mocked. If you give money with the wrong motivations, you will only reap corruption (Gal. 6:8). He loves a *cheerful* giver, someone who is happy to be a divine partner. But, if He can trust you, He'll bless you exceedingly.

Are you simply someone who gives, or are you a giver? A giver isn't simply defined by his acts of giving, but by the state of his heart toward God and toward God's Kingdom. A giver is one who is fulfilled when he gives. A giver is someone who takes more pleasure in giving than in receiving. Givers are qualified for partnership, and partners are promised prosperity!

God is looking for a few good men (and women) to entrust with wealth. Are you one of them?

"Thus saith the LORD, thy Redeemer, the Holy One of Israel; I am the Lord thy God which <u>teacheth thee to profit</u>, which leadeth thee by the way that thou shouldest go."
Isaiah 48:17 [emphasis mine]

9

The Man of God and Your Finances

Not many Christians currently understand the power of what you're going to learn in this chapter. In my own research, I quickly came to realize that this subject is a very important part of the prosperity message. The problem is that because of a secular idea called a "conflict of interest", many preachers are afraid to teach it.

My personal conviction is to throw this concept to the wind when it comes to teaching the word. I understand the need of such restrictions when it comes to secular issues, but when it comes to God's truth, I'm charged as a minister to "preach the word", to "be instant in season, out of season," and to teach "all doctrine" (2Ti. 4:2), not just the portion that won't present a conflict of interest. Shame on us for trading God's truth so as not to *risk* a conflict of interest. We **must** return to declaring the whole counsel of God! (Acts 20:27)

> **NOTE:** I'm going to use the term "man of God" in this chapter. But, understand that I'm using this phrase in the broad sense throughout—man *or* woman of God.

Let's delve into this important issue, an issue God has quite a bit to say about—the link between the man of God and your finances.

The Divine Exchange

"He that receiveth you receiveth me, and he that receiveth me receiveth him that sent me. [41] He that receiveth a prophet in the name of a prophet shall receive a prophet's reward; and he that receiveth a righteous man in the name of a righteous man shall receive a righteous man's reward. [42] And whosoever shall give to drink unto one of these little ones a cup of cold water only in the name of a disciple, verily I say unto you, he shall in no wise lose his reward."

Matthew 10:40-42

"That all men should honor the Son, even as they honor the Father. He that honoreth not the Son honoreth not the Father which hath sent him."

John 5:23

From these two passages, a very clear principle is established. When people receive or reject the person sent, they aren't simply receiving or rejecting that person. They're receiving or rejecting the one who sent him/her.

According to Jesus' statement in Matthew 10:40, this blessing connection reaches all the way back to the Father. When people receive (honor) the man of God whom Jesus has sent to minister the word, they are receiving (honoring) Christ Himself. But, it doesn't stop there. When they receive Christ, they're receiving the one who sent Him, as well—God, the Father. And what's amazing about this connection is that the blessing reserved for the man of God will also be poured out on those who honor him.

Now, what does it mean to *honor* the man of God, the one whom Christ sent? To answer that, let's look at a few passages that speak to that effect.

"Honor the LORD with thy substance, and with the firstfruits of all thine increase…"

Proverbs 3:9

"A son honoreth his father, and a servant his master: if then I be a father, where is mine honor? and if I be a master, where is my fear? saith the LORD of hosts unto you, O priests, that despise my name. And ye say, Wherein have we despised thy name? [7] Ye offer polluted bread upon mine altar; and ye say, Wherein have we polluted thee? In that ye say, The table of the LORD is contemptible. [8] And if ye offer the blind for sacrifice, is it not evil? and if ye offer the lame and sick, is it not evil? offer it now unto thy governor; will he be pleased with thee, or accept thy person?

saith the LORD of hosts."

Malachi 1:6-8

It's clear that when it comes to honoring God, He certainly isn't talking about saying, "Thank you Jesus." This is made very clear in the first passage (Prov. 3:9), which explicitly stated that we honor the Lord with our substance. In the second passage, it's obvious that financial substance is the object used to honor God when you consider how the people *dishonored* Him. God stated that they offered polluted bread upon His altar, and blemished cattle for sacrifice.

NOTE: As an agrarian society, wealth was offered to God by way of agricultural yield. Today, this translates into money.

The biblical reality is that one of the primary ways you honor/dishonor God is with your money. The amount you give to God, and the priority that giving has in your life determines whether God is honored or dishonored by your offering.

This selfsame principle applies when it comes to honoring the man of God.

"Let the elders that rule well be counted worthy of double honor, especially they who labor in the word and doctrine. [18] For the Scripture saith, Thou shalt not muzzle the ox that treadeth out the corn. And, The laborer is worthy of his reward."

1 Timothy 5:17-18

Yet again, we see the term "honor" being connected to financial gifts. What you must understand is how God intends for this "blessings chain" to operate. When you give to the man of God, you are making connection with a chain that links all the way back to the Father Himself. The blessing that God pours out on the man of God will be directed toward you *through* the very chain you got connected to through giving!

> *"And Melchizedek king of Salem brought forth bread and wine: and he was the priest of the most high God. [19] And he blessed him, and said, Blessed be Abram of the most high God, possessor of heaven and earth: [20] And blessed be the most high God, which hath delivered thine enemies into thy hand. And he gave him tithes of all."*
>
> Genesis 14:18-20

NOTE: This is one of two examples of pre-Law tithing. The other is found in Gen. 28:22.

In this passage, we see the divine exchange in action. The priest of God, King Melchizedek, went out to receive Abram after his battle with an alliance of kings (in which Abram was victorious). Melchizedek blessed Abram, and in response to the blessing Abram received, he gave to Melchizedek 10% of the spoils. Did you catch the exchange? Melchizedek blessed Abram with something spiritual, and Abram responded by blessing Melchizedek with something natural.

Here's another example of the principle of the divine exchange in action...

> *"And when they were come to the land of Zuph, Saul said*
> *to his servant that was with him, Come, and let us return;*
> *lest my father leave caring for the asses, and take thought for*
> *us. [6] And he said unto him, Behold now, there is in this*
> *city a man of God, and he is an honorable man; all that he*
> *saith cometh surely to pass: now let us go thither;*
> *peradventure he can show us our way that we should go. [7]*
> *Then said Saul to his servant, But, behold, if we go, what*
> *shall we bring the man? for the bread is spent in our vessels,*
> *and there is not a present to bring to the man of God: what*
> *have we?"*
>
> *1 Samuel 9:5-7*

Saul, who would eventually become the first king of Israel, understood this divine exchange very well. If you read from the beginning of the chapter, you'll see that Saul was out looking for his father's lost donkeys. But, he couldn't find them. So, the servant who was with Saul suggested they go and ask the man of God for directions.

Saul's response is key. You see, he understood that it was contrary to God's system to expect the man of God to bless him spiritually and for him not to be able to bless the man of God in return. Apparently, Saul understood how the divine exchange worked, and he didn't want to circumvent it. So, he told his servant, "We don't have a gift to give to the man of God, so it's not proper for us to go asking him to be a blessing to us."

Eventually, they came up with a gift and went and found the man of God, who was Samuel... and the rest is history.

This divine exchange is a principle that Paul taught quite explicitly in his epistles.

> *"Let him that is taught in the word communicate [give] unto him that teacheth in all good things. [7] Be not deceived; God is not mocked: for whatsoever a man soweth, that shall he also reap. [8] For he that soweth to his flesh shall of the flesh reap corruption; but he that soweth to the Spirit shall of the Spirit reap life everlasting. [9] And let us not be weary in well doing: for in due season we shall reap, if we faint not."*
>
> *Galatians 6:6-9*

Something many people do not realize is that this famous "you reap what you sow" passage was actually taught by Paul in the context of giving to the man of God, as you can see. That's the danger involved in taking a passage out of context. You lose the power of its original intent.

Considering the greater context of what Paul said in this passage, this would be a fairly accurate modern day representation of the text:

Those of you who are taught the word should give to the ones who teach. Don't be tricked by stinginess. God has a system in place, and He will make sure that whatever you give, you'll get. If you only care about satisfying your carnal needs, you'll receive corruption in return. But, if you give to the more valuable things of the Spirit, you'll reap everlasting life. And don't ever get tired of giving, even if you don't see immediate results, because in God's time, you'll receive your harvest, but only if you don't stop giving.

The Pastor Weekly Version

It's quite obvious how God feels about giving to the man of God, particularly those who teach you (both in your local church and in other teaching media, e.g. television, books, audio/video, websites, etc.). God considers it "well doing" when you sow seeds into the lives of those who bless you by sharing the word.

When faced with this truth, some people think of ways to get out of giving. First, they think, *Well, my pastor gets a salary from my church, and I give tithes and offerings to the church, so that's how I give to my pastor, albeit indirectly.* But, this isn't a true assertion at all. By virtue of the tithe, it doesn't belong to you anyway, so the Lord most certainly doesn't consider it something you gave to the man of God.

Secondly, even your offerings aren't yours once you give them to God through the agency of the Church. How can you take credit for what's done with money that you *gave* to God? The offering is not a profit-sharing investment program. Once you give it, it does not belong to you anymore, plain and simple. It's right that the institution of the Church provides salaries to the spiritual leadership, particularly to those who minister in the word. But, it's still important to God that *you* give to those who pour the word into your life, and He set up this chained-blessing system to ensure that you're blessed for your "well doing".

Something else people often think is, *Well, if I purchased the media (book, audio, video, etc.), I **did** give to the man of God by virtue of the fact that I made the purchase.* Again, this isn't true in the slightest. If you did purchase the media, you received value from the purchase, just as if you'd bought secular media. You don't consider the purchase of secular music as seed sowing, do you? So, why would you think that by purchasing media, you're actually planting a seed into the lives of ministers? A gift is a gift when value is not received in return. This is not applicable to purchases made for ministry products.

I hope that these thought patterns don't describe your way of thinking. If so, you have an opportunity to change that right now. Remember, God loves a "cheerful giver", not someone who's looking for any way to *not* give that they can find. It's not like God is mandating that you give (except maybe in the case of tithing, which technically isn't *giving* anyway). If you don't want to be a giver, that's your choice. But, for those who see God's heart and purpose in seed sowing and who choose to activate the principles involved, the blessing of financial prosperity is your promise.

The Scriptures say plenty about giving to the man of God. As a matter of fact, Paul committed a substantial amount of time to teaching it. He taught the Corinthians, Galatians (quoted above), Philippians, and his spiritual son, Timothy (quoted above) about this principle. Apparently, it isn't an issue that God takes lightly.

First, let's examine the Corinthian teaching, in which Paul gave an entire teaching on the subject, not just a passing mention.

"Am I not an apostle? am I not free? have I not seen Jesus Christ our Lord? are not ye my work in the Lord? [2] If I be not an apostle unto others, yet doubtless I am to you: for the seal of mine apostleship are ye in the Lord. [3] Mine answer to them that do examine me is this, [4] Have we not power to eat and to drink? [5] Have we not power to lead about a sister, a wife, as well as other apostles, and as the brethren of the Lord, and Cephas? [6] Or I only and Barnabas, have not we power to forbear working? [7] **Who goeth a warfare any time at his own charges? who planteth a vineyard, and eateth not of the fruit thereof? or who feedeth a flock, and eateth not of the milk of the flock?** *[8] Say I these things as a man? or saith not the law the same also? [9] For it is written in the law of Moses,* **Thou shalt not muzzle the mouth of the ox that treadeth out the corn.** *Doth God take care for oxen? [10] Or saith he it altogether for our sakes? For our sakes, no doubt, this is written: that he that ploweth should plow in hope; and that he that thresheth in hope should be partaker of his hope. [11]* **If we have sown unto you spiritual things, is it a great thing if we shall reap your carnal things?** *[12] If others be partakers of this power over you, are not we rather? Nevertheless we have not used this*

power; but suffer all things, lest we should hinder the gospel of Christ. [13] **Do ye not know that they which minister about holy things live of the things of the temple? and they which wait at the altar are partakers with the altar? [14] Even so hath the Lord ordained that they which preach the gospel should live of the gospel.** *[15] But I have used none of these things: neither have I written these things, that it should be so done unto me: for it were better for me to die, than that any man should make my glorying void. [16] For though I preach the gospel, I have nothing to glory of: for necessity is laid upon me; yea, woe is unto me, if I preach not the gospel! [17] For if I do this thing willingly, I have a reward: but if against my will, a dispensation of the gospel is committed unto me. [18] What is my reward then? Verily that, when I preach the gospel, I may make the gospel of Christ without charge, that I abuse not my power in the gospel. [19] For though I be free from all men, yet have I made myself servant unto all, that I might gain the more."*

1 Corinthians 9:1-19 [emphases mine]

I know this is a long quotation, but it's important that you see the entire context of Paul's discourse. The portions I have in bold demonstrate clearly that those who minister the gospel are supposed to reap of the people they minister to. In other words, the ministers are the sowers, the word is the seed, and the congregation is the field.

189

So, if the ministers have sown the word ("spiritual things") into the field, they're supposed to reap the harvest of the people's money or other gifts ("carnal things").

Paul asks, "What soldier goes to war on behalf of the nation and then has to pay for it himself?" That's a good question, and the answer is that the people he fights for are supposed to pay. He also asks, "Who plants crops or raises cattle and doesn't receive something from the field of his labor?" He's obviously saying that it's not right for a man of God to so diligently sow the word into people's lives and reap no material harvest from the fields in which they sow.

The fourteenth verse makes it clear that giving to the man of God (both through Church salary and through individual giving) is God's own setup. It says that God has **ordained** that those who preach the gospel should "live of the gospel." In other words, leadership in Christian ministry (particularly, those who preach and teach the word) should have their living off of the gospel. They should **not** be made to hold down fulltime secular employment.

Now, because of the conflict of interest such teachings pose (and why many preachers today refuse to teach it), Paul makes sure he tells the people in verse 15 that although what he has taught is right (and is God's divine setup – v. 14), he's not telling them just so they'd give more to him.

He spent the rest of this passage ensuring that people didn't think he was teaching this just so they'd give more. It's a shame he even had to go into that, but knowing how so many Christians think (especially when it comes to money matters), I understand his need to have done so.

"But I rejoiced in the Lord greatly, that now at the last your
care of me hath flourished again; wherein ye were also
careful, but ye lacked opportunity. [11] Not that I speak in
respect of want: for I have learned, in whatsoever state I am,
therewith to be content. [12] I know both how to be abased,
and I know how to abound: every where and in all things I
am instructed both to be full and to be hungry, both to
abound and to suffer need. [13] I can do all things through
Christ which strengtheneth me. [14] Notwithstanding ye
have well done, that ye did communicate with my affliction.
[15] Now ye Philippians know also, that in the beginning
of the gospel, when I departed from Macedonia, no church
communicated with me as concerning giving and receiving,
but ye only. [16] For even in Thessalonica ye sent once and
again unto my necessity. [17] Not because I desire a gift:
but I desire fruit that may abound to your account. [18] But
I have all, and abound: I am full, having received of
Epaphroditus the things which were sent from you, an odor
of a sweet smell, a sacrifice acceptable, well-pleasing to God.
[19] But my God shall supply all your need according to his
riches in glory by Christ Jesus."

Philippians 4:10-19

It's amazing how many people are very quick to quote verse 19, but never even begin to consider the context in which that blessing was pronounced. This blessing of supplying was pronounced as a direct result of the Philippians' liberality in giving to Paul. He said that they had "done well", in that they gave to him during his time of affliction (v. 14).

Now, look at the horrible shame of the Christian churches in verses 15-16. As Paul traveled, preaching the gospel, only the Philippian church planted seeds into his life and ministry. Even while he preached in Thessalonica, it was the Philippians who sent money to him over and over again.

Even today, it seems like Christians just don't like the idea of giving money to the man of God. As I stated before, they're quick to talk about the fact that the pastor already gets a salary, or that they planted a seed when they purchased a media product, but that's not the heart of a giver. These Philippians were givers. Even when Paul had left their city, they **sent** money to wherever he was ministering at the time. They appreciated the fact that this man of God had poured spiritual seed into their ground, and they showed their love and appreciation by giving to him over and over again (so that others around the world could be blessed by Paul's continued ministry).

Notice, the Philippians didn't say, "Well, now that Paul is in Thessalonica, it's *their* responsibility to give to him." They weren't looking for a way to *not* give. They were committed to blessing the man of God. They understood God's principles, and they were a shining example of how we should be today.

Something else many people don't realize is that God is so serious about this issue of giving to the man of God that He's keeping a divine record of every seed you sow (v. 17). There's an account in Heaven that's being kept regarding you, and when you sow seeds in the man of God's life, the fruit of those seeds sown are added to your account. I don't know about you, but that's good news to me.

And once again, we see Paul making sure to deal with the possible perception of a conflict of interest. In verses 11-13 and 17, he emphasizes that he's not trying to *get* anything out of them, but rather, just trying to teach them the spiritual principles surrounding their acts of love and giving.

I'm glad Paul honored the word enough to teach this issue even though a conflict of interest existed. I applaud him, because had he shied away from the subject like so many preachers do today, the Church would be much more at a loss regarding God's purposes in seed sowing and financial prosperity, and regarding the connection between the man of God and your finances. Thank you, Paul!

News At 11: Prophet Takes Widow's Last

"And the word of the LORD came unto him, saying, [9] Arise, get thee to Zarephath, which belongeth to Zidon, and dwell there: behold, I have commanded a widow woman there to sustain thee. [10] So he arose and went to Zarephath. And when he came to the gate of the city, behold, the widow woman was there gathering of sticks: and he called to her, and said, Fetch me, I pray thee, a little water in a vessel, that I may drink. [11] And as she was going to fetch it, he called to her, and said, Bring me, I pray thee, a morsel of bread in thine hand. [12] And she said, As the LORD thy God liveth, I have not a cake, but a handful of meal in a barrel, and a little oil in a cruse: and, behold, I am gathering two sticks, that I may go in and dress it for me

and my son, that we may eat it, and die. [13] And Elijah
said unto her, Fear not; go and do as thou hast said: but
make me thereof a little cake first, and bring it unto me,
and after make for thee and for thy son. [14] For thus saith
the LORD God of Israel, The barrel of meal shall not
waste, neither shall the cruse of oil fail, until the day that the
LORD sendeth rain upon the earth. [15] And she went
and did according to the saying of Elijah: and she, and he,
and her house, did eat many days. [16] And the barrel of
meal wasted not, neither did the cruse of oil fail, according to
the word of the LORD, which he spoke by Elijah."

1 Kings 17:8-16

This is a very interesting narrative. Here, a poor widow
woman was about to make a small last meal for herself and her son so
that they could eat it and die. She told this to the man of God (Elijah)
and look at how he responded. Rather than saying, "First, come over
here so I can lay hands and pray for you," he said something that
carnal-minded people would consider absolutely treacherous, selfish,
greedy, and corrupt. He said, "Before you make the little bit that you
have left for you and your son, make me some…" In effect, this
would leave the widow with even less than what little she already had.

Can you imagine how people today would respond to such a
thing happening? The news media would be all over it. It would
headline the prime time news, radio, and newspapers. And to be
honest, looking from their carnal perspective, it *would* seem like a
horrible thing to instruct this poor woman to do. *Talk about a conflict of*

interest!

Even today, the media loves to do so-called exposés on prosperity preachers, casting them in as horrible a light as they possibly can. Now, I'm not saying that there isn't such a thing as a crooked minister, or a crooked ministry. What I *am* saying, however, is that we can't be so carnal-minded that we don't activate the divine exchange in our lives. Give to *any* ministry? Absolutely not. But give, nonetheless.

Now, the power of this story is not found in Elijah's instruction to the widow, but rather, in her response. She didn't call him a thieving bastard and tell him where he could put his prophecy. No, she went and did what he instructed her to do. And because she became a partner in the divine exchange by honoring the man of God, she harvested a steady stream of increase that outlasted the drought that was ravishing the region.

When the blessing of God is on you, you'll be the only one standing when everyone around you is going through. You'll be the only one with oil flowing while others are begging for rain. That's exactly what God promised would happen in Malachi 3:12, when He said that even the heathens would recognize that you were blessed!

Let's look at this story of Elijah and the widow from the spiritual standpoint. All that small cake would have bought her and her son would have been another day or so. Its only power was to satiate their hunger for a short while. It wasn't as though the food was going to fix her problem. Thankfully, rather than consuming it for herself, she took a leap of faith and planted it as a seed into the life of an anointed man of God. She made the divine connection, and God

195

blessed her abundantly.

Activate The Exchange

The principle of giving to the man of God is a very practical step you should take to activate the promises of prosperity in your life. It's not something that you need to dwell on for months and months. You need to simply make a decision to grab hold to the spirit of the system God has set up and enter into this partnership.

In your local church, when your pastor preaches a message that is a blessing to you (whether through encouragement, correction, instruction, or even rebuke), you should sow a seed into him. Don't forget that you make a divine connection when you do that, and God's blessing on His life flows to you through that connection.

You may notice that in many churches, people walk up and put money on the altar (or pulpit stairs) during the sermon. I can't guarantee that in every case it's the same, but my assumption is that the money put on the altar goes to the man of God who's teaching at that time. These believers are giving directly to the man of God (not just to the church), planting a seed into his life at the moment the anointing is flowing. They're smart enough to make the divine connection and allow the blessing of God to flow through that man of God and into their own lives. It's right and good, and such offerings arise to God as a sweet-smelling savor (Ph. 4:18).

When you watch television ministries and they are a blessing to your life, you should give to those ministries. In addition, you should send gifts directly to the man of God who ministered. The same should be the case when you frequent a Bible teachings website, or purchase a teaching book, or an audio/video tape/disc. Basically, whenever a teacher of the word ministers to you spiritually, you should minister to him or her financially.

One word of wisdom before I conclude this chapter… As a pastor, I have seen many times when someone hears a message, gets excited, responds to it in faith, and continues in it for about 2 weeks (if for that long). But afterward, it's back to business as usual. Don't simply put these principles in action in the here and now and forget about them later. Remember, the windows of Heaven don't open up after just one act of well doing, but after consistency and faithfulness is shown. Put this in your heart and you'll continue in it.

Partner with God by partnering with His ministers. As they pour into your life, pour into theirs. As you drink from the well of their labor in the word, deposit back into that well with your gifts. This is the heart of God, His divine setup—the way He intended for ministry to work. Take advantage of the connection between the man of God and your finances, and watch God's blessing of supply (Ph. 4:19) manifest in your life.

"But I have all, and abound: I am full, having received of Epaphroditus the things which were sent from you, an odor of a sweet smell, a sacrifice acceptable, well-pleasing to God."
Philippians 4:18 [emphasis mine]

Section Four

Principles That Govern Prosperity

I n the previous section, we examined the basics of how God's financial system operates. We defined the system itself, and examined His established methods of tapping into its power. In this section, we're going to build on this groundwork by delving into the principles that actually fuel the system's efficacy in your life.

Ultimately, we'll be dealing with the difference between wisdom and knowledge. Understanding that there *is* a system, and even knowing how to work it is quite different from comprehending the principles that drive it.

Consider computers… While you may know how to operate one, a computer scientist can make it do things you never imagined possible. Why? —Because he understands not only how to operate the machine itself, but also comprehends the principles that allow it to do what it does.

Amateurs know how to work a system. Professionals know how the system works! In the same way, only when you know the principles that govern God's economic system can you make it work for you to the fullest.

10

Financial Stewardship

God has established principles that govern how the prosperity system works, the cornerstone of which is financial stewardship. Without a firm grasp of this principle, wealth will not only be fleeting, but it will also be a stumbling block to your spiritual walk.

In the King James Version of the Bible, the Greek word translated as "steward" is the word *oikonomos*. It is translated as "someone employed in the capacity of a manager or overseer, particularly as it relates to fiscal matters." It's from *oikonomos* that we get the modern English word "economy", which is "the system of production, distribution, and consumption".

So, stewardship is a *system* that God has set up to govern our finances. It's His set of principles that are supposed to govern the *production* of wealth, the *distribution* (usage) of wealth, and the *consumption* of wealth in our lives. That's a powerful statement, so I hope you understand it.

We're going to examine financial stewardship in this chapter, but I want to be clear that these are not suggestions for wealthy living. I don't intend to provide you with inspirational rhetoric or guidelines that it would simply *benefit* you to follow. The whole idea of stewardship is that we are under the employment of God. We have been "hired" to oversee (manage) the wealth He has put into our hands. This being the case, there are rules to follow—guidelines established by the Giver that govern our employment.

> *"Moreover it is **required** in stewards, that a man be found faithful."*
> 1 Corinthians 4:2 [emphasis mine]

If we are to be found faithful, we have no choice but to master this stewardship principle.

> *"He that is faithful in that which is least is faithful also in much: and he that is unjust in the least is unjust also in much. [11] If therefore ye have not been faithful in the unrighteous mammon, who will commit to your trust the true riches?"*
> Luke 16:10-11

I'm always amazed at how many people actually expect God to bless them with increase when they've shown little to no faithfulness over what God has already given them. Being a child of God is not enough to warrant abundance and overflow. You must demonstrate to God that you'll be faithful and ***then*** increase will come.

"He said therefore, A certain noble man went into a far country to receive for himself a kingdom, and to return. [13] And he called his ten servants, and delivered them ten pounds, and said unto them, Occupy till I come. [14] But his citizens hated him, and sent a message after him, saying, We will not have this man to reign over us. [15] And it came to pass, that when he was returned, having received the kingdom, then he commanded these servants to be called unto him, to whom he had given the money, that he might know how much every man had gained by trading. [16] Then came the first, saying, Lord, thy pound hath gained ten pounds. [17] And he said unto him, Well, thou good servant: because thou hast been faithful in a very little, have thou authority over ten cities. [18] And the second came, saying, Lord, thy pound hath gained five pounds. [19] And he said likewise to him, Be thou also over five cities. [20] And another came, saying, Lord, behold, here is thy pound, which I have kept laid up in a napkin: [21] For I feared thee, because thou art an austere man: thou takest up that thou laidst not down, and reapest that thou didst not sow. [22] And he saith unto him, Out of thine own mouth will I judge thee, thou wicked servant. Thou knewest that I was an austere man, taking up that I laid not down, and reaping that I did not sow: [23] Wherefore then gavest not thou my money into the bank, that at my coming I might have

required mine own with usury? [24] And he said unto them
that stood by, Take from him the pound, and give it to him
that hath ten pounds. [25] (And they said unto him, Lord,
he hath ten pounds.) [26] For I say unto you, That unto
every one which hath shall be given; and from him that hath
not, even that he hath shall be taken away from him."

Luke 19:12-26

In this passage, Jesus tells a parable to His disciples. Parables were always fictional stories that Jesus used to illustrate spiritual truths. This passage is actually a goldmine of principles that will help us get a clear understanding of how this whole *stewardship* thing works.

NOTE: Through the remainder of this chapter, I'll be referring often to this passage (Luke 19:12-26) as the "stewardship passage".

Principle #1: You Don't Own *Anything*

The first principle that governs stewardship is not simply first in numeric sequence. It's the umbrella principle that blankets all the others. What is this principle?

You don't own anything.

The stewardship passage lays this principle out in verse 13, and it's actually pretty easy to overlook it. The verse states that the nobleman "delivered" or entrusted his servants with various amounts of money. The implication, of course, is that he was entrusting them with his own money, and that the servants, although recipients of the money, were expected to deal faithfully with what belonged to the master.

Child of God, don't be tricked. You don't really own the clothes on your back, the house you live in (and neither does the mortgage company—no matter what they tell you), or even the money in your bank account. That's not always an easy admission to make, but the truth has the uncanny ability to free us from our misconceptions. But, having admitted this truth, to whom does everything belong?

> *"...The earth is the LORD's, and the fullness thereof; the*
> *world, and they that dwell therein."*
>
> *Psalms 24:1*

If you don't understand anything else, you **must** grasp the notion that God owns the world and everything in it. You have been made a steward of all that He has entrusted to you. But, don't forget your place. Everything in your possession belongs to God, and you must act accordingly.

When it comes to making decisions with your money, you can't let the sole determination be your opinion, your emotions, your experiences, or your plans. How dare a steward deal selfishly with what doesn't belong to him in the first place?

Once you realize you don't own anything, it should totally change your perception of wealth (and of all your belongings). All of a sudden, you realize that all that you've achieved and obtained isn't because you were so smart or so wise. In fact, you didn't even get what you have by being *lucky*. God simply chose to entrust you with His belongings, and if nothing else humbles you, that revelation should.

Whether you have little or much, you're simply a steward, a distribution center for God. Even when you are moved from little to much and are walking in wealth, you're still just a distribution center. Despite the size of your estate, it all belongs to God and must be used as He determines.

When you're entrusted with something that doesn't belong to you, you're expected to use it only for the purposes for which it was given in the first place. In most cases, violation of this usually unspoken requirement results in you no longer being trusted again; and once trust is lost, it's a very difficult thing to rebuild.

You **must** understand that having something in your possession does not imply that you have been given free reign over it. Having possession of money doesn't imply that you can do with it as you please. Even if you have millions, you can't just use them for your own gratification and expect God to be pleased. He has set up a system of laws that govern a steward's management of wealth. You must be faithful to that system. You must be found a faithful steward over what belongs to God.

Because our wealth belongs to God, we represent Him in our usage of it. If we profess God, but use wealth in a way that is not in line with His purposes, we are misrepresenting Him to all who see it. So, we must be very careful to manage God's money in such a way that glory and not shame is brought to Him or to His Church.

All of a sudden, wealth becomes a responsibility... a burden to bear; and in truth, that's exactly what it is—at least, that's what it is to the faithful steward. Because of this responsibility, the temptations associated with wealth are great. But, temptation should **never** dictate your willingness to glorify God. Knowing that He wants you wealthy should be enough for you to receive it, and to use it in a way that demonstrates that it's His and not your own.

Principle #2: You Are Accountable To The Master

"So then every one of us shall give account of himself to
God."

Romans 14:12

In the free world, personal accountability is a virtue that seems to have faded into memory. Unfortunately, this has resulted in a hedonistic approach to decision-making. But as Christians, we must never forget that no matter how free we are in our current nations, we are but pilgrims here. Our citizenship is in Heaven, and we are absolutely accountable to our Heavenly Father and King.

Let's take a look at a portion of the stewardship passage and see what it reveals about accountability.

"And it came to pass, that when he was returned, having
received the kingdom, then he commanded these servants to

be called unto him, to whom he had given the money, that he
might know how much every man had gained by trading."

Luke 19:15

When the Lord Jesus returns, you will have to give an account
for what you have done with all that He has entrusted to your care
and keeping. It's a serious responsibility to be a steward, and if you
want to be found faithful in His eyes, you must make His direction
regarding your finances an unchallenged authority in your life.

Principle #3: You *Can* Handle What He Gives You

Listen, saint of God. If God gives you $400,000,000 ($400
million), you have it within you to be a good steward over it. It's not
as though a lot of money automatically produces crooked morality or
greed. When you are unfaithful, it's because you made a choice to be,
not because the weight of the responsibility was too much for you to
handle.

"There hath no temptation taken you but such as is common
to man: but God is faithful, who will not suffer you to be
tempted above that ye are able; but will with the temptation
also make a way to escape, that ye may be able to bear it."

1 Corinthians 10:13

Money isn't the culprit when one makes bad decisions.
Actually, money is neither good nor bad, moral nor immoral. It is an

impersonal object that can be used for both good and bad purposes. It's totally inert until it's put to use in one way or the other.

People often quote First Timothy 6:10 as saying, "Money is the root of all evil," but it would serve you well to revisit that passage.

*"For **the love of** money is the root of all evil: which while some coveted after, they have erred from the faith, and pierced themselves through with many sorrows."*
1 Timothy 6:10 [emphasis mine]

Sometimes, Christians have excuses for everything. But, wouldn't it be great if we could go to God when we fall short and simply say, "Lord, I messed up. I really missed the mark and it was nobody's fault but mine. I can't even blame the devil because he was doing his job. I just wasn't doing mine."

Instead, we often say something along the lines of, "Lord, I was so tempted, and I just couldn't handle it…" Sometimes we say this with our mouths, and sometimes we say it with our attitudes and actions. Either way, it shouldn't be our response when we falter. It's not about what we can or cannot handle, it's about our choices, and nobody's responsible for those choices but us.

Such thinking reminds me of Adam and Eve. Rather than to take responsibility for his actions (eating of the forbidden fruit), Adam blamed it on Eve. When God turned to Eve for an explanation, she blamed it on the serpent. It would have been great if Adam would have simply said, "Lord, you told me not to do it, and I did it anyway. I'm so sorry."

> *"For the kingdom of heaven is as a man traveling into a far*
> *country, who called his own servants, and delivered unto*
> *them his goods. [15] And unto one he gave five talents, to*
> *another two, and to another one; to every man*
> ***according to his several ability****; and*
> *straightway took his journey."*
> *Matthew 25:14-15 [emphasis mine]*

When we understand that God won't put more on us than we're able to handle, we have no recourse but to take responsibility for our sins. When we are unfaithful stewards, it's not because we had more than we could handle. It's because we *chose* not to handle it, whether directly or indirectly.

If you skip a tithe, for example, it's not because your electric bill is due. It's not because your car is about it get repossessed. It's simply because you *choose* not to tithe. Certain things in your life may affect your decision, but the reality is that the electric bill doesn't force you to not tithe. Food in your children's mouths doesn't force you to not tithe. (I know I'm going to get hate mail on that one, but I meant to say exactly what I said.) It's all about choices, and as a steward over what doesn't belong to you, you must be found faithful.

Here's a saying I really love: If God brought you *to* it, He'll bring you *through* it. There's nothing you're faced with that God won't provide the "way of escape", but you have to make a conscious choice to bear it, and to continue to be faithful through it. Only then will you empower God to not only *provide* an open door, but to lead you through it.

What's the moral of the story? Stewards don't make excuses for failure. They repent and start making the right choices from then on. They don't hide behind the *appearance* of a bad situation, claiming that the situation forced them to deal treacherously. They face it head-on, knowing that somewhere in the darkness is a way of escape. Stewards are faithful to the Master, and He is faithful to them!

And by the way, don't be afraid of wealth. Don't be intimidated by the thought that you can finally have more than enough. You won't be overwhelmed, and you won't be unfaithful unless you choose to. You *can* handle wealth, so go ahead and receive it and let God be glorified in you, by you, and through you.

Principle #4: Motivations Matter

I have a question for you…

Why do you want to be wealthy?

I can't overemphasize the importance of the answer to this question. You **will not** have longevity in your experience of prosperity if your reasons for pursuing it are ungodly. In addition, your motivations are an indication of whether or not you have it in yourself to remain faithful in your stewardship even when faced with very strong temptations to do otherwise (and I don't care who you are, you **will** be tempted to do otherwise).

Unfortunately, a major problem is embedded just beneath the

surface of this question, a problem that has the power to make the answer absolutely meaningless. So, you really need to deal with the problem before even pondering the answer.

The Problem: Christians have become masters of religion. We know what to say, when to say it, and how to say it. We've programmed ourselves to say the "right" things and to feign absolute spiritual integrity. That may *sound* good, and in religion, it may actually *be* good, but Christianity is **not** a religion. It is the expression of God's love. And in this "expression", it's not the *form* of godliness that holds the power of our faith (2Ti. 3:5). It's the truth (Jn. 8:32).

So, when considering the answer to this question, do away with the years of programming you've received from church culture. Don't give the answer that sounds good. Take an honest, introspective look and simply be truthful both to yourself and to God.

Do you want to be wealthy so you can have enough clothes to go a month without repeating? Do you want to be wealthy so you can quit your job, hire a maid, and lay around watching television all day? Whatever your reasons for wanting to be wealthy, you simply **must** be honest... It's the truth that makes you free; so don't hide from it. Only then can you make your motivations right if they aren't already.

If this book is going to help you at all, it's imperative you understand that your motivations matter deeply. If your motivations are out of kilter, so will be your management of wealth. If your motivations are and remain godly, on the other hand, you'll never have to worry about being led astray by personal ambitions.

Always keep in mind that while you may have mastered the look and speech of a Christian, God isn't much concerned about what's on the outside.

> *"But the LORD said unto Samuel, 'Look not on his countenance, or on the height of his stature; because I have refused him: for the LORD seeth not as man seeth; for man looketh on the outward appearance, but the LORD looketh on the heart.'"*
>
> *1 Samuel 16:7*

> *"But this I say, He which soweth sparingly shall reap also sparingly; and he which soweth bountifully shall reap also bountifully. [7] Every man according as he purposeth in his heart, so let him give; not grudgingly, or of necessity: for God loveth a cheerful giver."*
>
> *2 Corinthians 9:6-7*

Notice in this second passage that after Paul stated that the bountiful sower would reap bountifully, he immediately dealt with the issue of motives. He understood that although it was true and worth stating that the bountiful sower would reap a bountiful return, the sower's motivations in giving were of vital importance. It does no good to give just because you want to receive.

Your giving should be cheerful—motivated out of love, not out of a vain desire to receive a return (even though that's the promise to those who give with the right motives). Anything else would make God's economy no better than a religious stock market, and offerings would be nothing more than a system of investing.

Keep in mind that motivations aren't some transcendent

emotional quality that you have no ability to control. Simply make a decision that you want to be wealthy so that you can be all the more useful to God (and don't think for a moment that poverty doesn't limit people's ability in this regard).

Wealth just doesn't matter if it's not used to glorify God. So, do yourself a favor and get your heart right at *this* stage rather than down the line, after repenting for making bad choices. Start to see money for what it actually is: Nothing but a tool useful to advance the purposes of God; and remember from Chapter 2 that the three purposes of wealth, in order of their priority, are: Kingdom advancement, benevolence, and *then* personal enjoyment.

Principle #5: Riches and Responsibilities Are Twins

I absolutely understand the predilection for assuming that riches can produce a lessening of responsibilities. One of the first things people think about when they picture themselves filthy rich is that they'll never have to go to work again. Well, let's just clear that misconception up right here and right now.

I have no interest in looking at riches from the world's perspective. From *God's* perspective, riches are **never** unaccompanied. With abundance of money comes an abundance of responsibility. God expects more of those who have more resources at their disposal; and when you think about it, that's not unreasonable.

"And that servant, which knew his lord's will, and prepared
not himself, neither did according to his will, shall be beaten

with many stripes. [48] But he that knew not, and did
commit things worthy of stripes, shall be beaten with few
stripes. For unto whomsoever much is given, of him shall be
much required: and to whom men have committed much, of
him they will ask the more."

Luke 12:47-48

If you're lazy and only want to get rich so you can shirk all your responsibilities and become a free spirit, think again! As a wealthy person, God will require more of you, plain and simple. If that's not what you had in mind, I'm not sure whether to tell you to stop reading here and donate this book to someone else, or to keep reading in the hopes that something I say will change your way of thinking. I'll let you decide which option better suits you. Let it suffice to say that if you're wealthy, the One who made you wealthy will expect you to put that wealth to proper use.

But Pastor, what types of responsibilities are we talking about here? Good question. First of all, you'll have a responsibility to be a substantial contributor to Christian ministry, whether to your local church, or to other ministries that are in the field doing a good work for the Kingdom.

In addition, wealthy people are given more scrutiny in our society. That being the case, wealthy Christians are particularly targeted by secular society because the world, by nature, loves to expose Christians who fail to live up to their Christian ideals, especially as it relates to financial matters. So, as a wealthy Christian, you'll have more people looking for you to fail or to lie and cheat. The preventative medicine for any such condition is integrity. More on that to come…

Finally, and most importantly, you will be expected to give all of your wealth away at the drop of a hat if God were to require it. The last thing you want is for your money to become a stumbling block to your faith-walk, because that's what's most important. Don't be like the rich ruler who, although he wanted to follow Christ, couldn't part with his wealth.

> *"And a certain ruler asked him, saying, Good Master, what shall I do to inherit eternal life? [19] And Jesus said unto him, Why callest thou me good? None is good, save one, that is, God. [20] Thou knowest the commandments, Do not commit adultery, Do not kill, Do not steal, Do not bear false witness, Honor thy father and thy mother. [21] And he said, All these have I kept from my youth up. [22] Now when Jesus heard these things, he said unto him, Yet lackest thou one thing: sell all that thou hast, and distribute unto the poor, and thou shalt have treasure in heaven: and come, follow me. [23] And when he heard this, he was very sorrowful: for he was very rich."*
>
> *Luke 18:18-23*

It's very easy to read this passage and get self-righteous, but I actually felt sorry for the man. He wasn't a phony. He truly wanted to follow Christ. His mistake, though, was that he was too attached to his wealth. Notice in verse 23 that he was sorrowful at Jesus' response. An uncaring man wouldn't have given Jesus a second

216

thought, but this man was hurt. He just couldn't part with what meant the most to him.

The moral of this story is not that Jesus is against His disciples having money, but that if you want to be His disciple, you have to be willing to part with whatever means the most to you. Had this man been poor but very connected to his family, I believe Jesus would have told him that if he followed, he'd have to leave his family behind. The whole point was to show this man that if he wanted to be a disciple, nothing could matter more than the Lord—a truth that we need to be reminded of today. (Luke 14:26)

Principle #6: Faith Is Essential

Stewardship has but one purpose: to please the Master. It's not about benefiting the steward or making life easy for him/her. It's about being faithful over the Master's goods so that when we give an account of ourselves, He's pleased with the job we've done. Considering this purpose, you cannot ignore the necessity of faith in your stewardship.

> *"But without faith it is impossible to please him..."*
> *Hebrews 11:6a*

You can't misinterpret this passage. It's **impossible** to please God without faith, plain and simple. So, if your goal in being a faithful steward is to please God, you have no choice but to make faith the primary determinant in your decision-making process.

"For we walk by faith, not by sight"

2 Corinthians 5:7

Although I will deal with exercising faith in your finances in more detail later on, it's important to emphasize the role that faith plays in your stewardship. If you're making decisions based on what you see, how you feel, or what everyone else is doing, you're not going to please God, even if the end result is that you're increased. What pleases God is when you choose to walk in accordance with His word, despite how your situations and circumstances dictate contradictory courses of action.

Would God require you to make decisions even though the result could be the loss of your job, the loss of your home, the loss of your car, your children going hungry, or other negative results? Absolutely! Just ask the rich young ruler in Luke 18:18-23, or Jesus' audience in Luke 14:25-35.

It amazes me how many people simply don't understand the whole concept of faith. If it makes sense to do certain things, and if you can see how the decision would logically produce positive results, where's the faith? If all the pieces are in place and it's never anything but obvious what you should do, where's the faith? Faith, by definition, is the evidence of things "not seen", meaning even when you don't have evidence, you should still proceed in obedience to God's direction.

Now, what I'm **not** saying is to make bad, uninformed decisions and call it faith. What I'm saying here is that when God has

218

provided you with direction, you don't need any other questions answered. "Lord, what would you have me do," is the only question a man of faith needs to have the answer to.

If your faith wavers when you're faced with situations that all but demand you do something that you know is not God's will, you **must** deny yourself the right to make your own decision. When your decision would be ungodly, simply refuse to make it on the basis that you own nothing anyway. Choose to be God's vessel and do what He tells you to do, come what may.

Now, the promise from God to a faithful steward is that you'll be increased. But, that doesn't mean that getting to that place will be an easy process. You must remember that faith isn't faith until you can't see how it's going to work out. Be a **faith**ful steward and trust God to have told you what is right. In the end, remember that it's not your right to make decisions contrary to what He's commanded, because everything you have belongs to Him anyway. Let that be your utmost conviction.

Principle #7: There's No Substitute For Hard Work

The last thing you should do is expect to sit back and watch your bank account fill with money because you pay your tithes and give in the offering. One principle that firmly governs God's brand of prosperity is that there's no substitute for hard work. Unfortunately, so many people want an easy way to wealth these days. God's plan, however, is quite different.

*"Wealth gotten by vanity shall be diminished: but he that
gathereth by labor shall increase."*

Proverbs 13:11

*"In all labor there is profit: but the talk of the lips tendeth
only to penury."*

Proverbs 14:23

God's not interested in making you wealthy for the heck of it. If that were the case, He'd cause His children to enter and win sweepstakes and giveaways all the time. But apparently, this is one of the rare cases in which the means are more valuable than the end.

You learn a lot when you generate wealth through the labor of your hands. Primarily, you learn to value money. That's one of the big problems with rich children whose parents never make them earn their way. When you don't value money (value, not treasure), you're likely to run out quickly.

Those who expect to *give* their way to millions have another thing coming. In fact, God feels so strongly about working that He said through the apostle Paul that if a man doesn't work, he shouldn't eat.

Now, I'm not saying that God demands that you hold down traditional secular employment. Even if you're working for ministry, that's honorable labor and valuable to the Kingdom. What I *am* saying, however, is that God expects you to work, and there's no way around that. Laziness is not of God.

Principle #8: Faithfulness Is Rewarded, and the Opposite Is Equally True

God is God, and we are His servants… Agree? This being the case, it's His prerogative as to how He responds to faithfulness. Because He's God, we couldn't (or rather, shouldn't) gripe if He decided not to reward faithfulness, nor could we cry injustice.

What's so wonderful about God, though, is that despite the fact that He's not compelled to do anything for His faithful servants, it's simply not in His character to overlook our labor of love. We serve a God who loves to reward His faithful stewards, and His promise is to always do just that.

> *"For God is not unrighteous to forget your work and labor*
> *of love, which ye have showed toward his name, in that ye*
> *have ministered to the saints, and do minister."*
>
> *Hebrews 6:10*

When you do the right thing, people may or may not know it; and even among those who know it, they may or may not acknowledge it. In contrast, the promise you have from God is that He won't forget your faithfulness. When you do the right thing, He adds it to your account (Ph. 4:17). He is keeping a record of all that you do as a steward, and He *will* reward you for your faithfulness.

> *"That thine alms may be in secret: and thy Father which*
> *seeth in secret himself shall reward thee openly."*
>
> *Matthew 6:4*

> *"But he shall receive a hundredfold now in this time, houses,*
> *and brethren, and sisters, and mothers, and children, and*
> *lands, with persecutions; and in the world to come eternal*
> *life."*
>
> *Mark 10:30*

These passages indicate that God will reward faithful stewards in *this* life. In the here and now, your Master will reward you if you are faithful over all that He has entrusted to you. What a joyous hope and expectation, knowing that although we aren't faithful just so we'll be rewarded, our God still desires to bless us *because* we're faithful.

But, not only will God reward us in this life, but He'll also reward us in the life to come. The following portion of the stewardship passage echoes words that I long to hear God say to me, words that I literally sit back and daydream about hearing Him say.

> *"And he said unto him, Well, thou good servant: because*
> *thou hast been faithful in a very little, have thou authority*
> *over ten cities."*
>
> *Luke 19:17*

The thought that God the omnipotent, God the marvelous would look at little ol' me and consider my service to Him a job well done… that's what I live for. Even as I write this, I'm humbled beyond words at the notion that God could be so pleased with me. It is my hope that you share in this humility, because it's a great motivator in being steadfast, unmovable, and abounding in the work of the Lord—knowing that your labor is not in vain. (1 Co. 15:58)

Now, as wonderful as these promises of reward are, many contemporary churches make the mistake of only teaching people about the rewards for faithfulness and totally (or in large part) ignoring the punishments for unfaithfulness. What a horrible treason.

While the good news is GREAT news, we must not forget that there are also negative implications of our faith-walk. Let's not just tell people that Heaven is wonderful. Let's remember to tell them that Hell is horrible. Let's not just deal with the rewards of faithfulness, but also with the punishments that accompany unfaithfulness.

If we examine the entirety of the stewardship passage, we'll see that faithfulness wasn't the only thing that provoked a response from the master.

"And another came, saying, Lord, behold, here is thy pound, which I have kept laid up in a napkin: [21] For I feared thee, because thou art an austere man: thou takest up that thou laidst not down, and reapest that thou didst not sow. [22] And he saith unto him, Out of thine own mouth will I judge thee, thou wicked servant. Thou knewest that I was an austere man, taking up that I laid not down, and reaping that I did not sow: [23] Wherefore then gavest not thou my money into the bank, that at my coming I might have required mine own with usury? [24] And he said unto them that stood by, Take from him the pound, and give it to

him that hath ten pounds."

Luke 19:20-24

If I focused solely on the reward to the faithful, I would be correct, but incomplete in my examination. In order to get the balance, we must recognize that God also punishes those who do not deal faithfully in their stewardship charge.

Consider an important point in this passage. One thing I've found through experience is that Christians are notorious for always having an excuse as to why they didn't do what they were supposed to do. Yet, when standing before the master, the unfaithful servant's excuse didn't actually *excuse* him. Far then from being an excuse, it was simply a *reason* he didn't do what he was supposed to do—and it didn't help him in the end.

Think back to Principle #3, which explains that you can handle whatever God gives you. If you can handle what He gives you, there are no excuses when you don't. If He wouldn't put more on you than you can bear, there's nothing you can say that justifies you when you have to give the accounting for your stewardship.

"And cast ye the unprofitable servant into outer darkness:
there shall be weeping and gnashing of teeth."

Matthew 25:30

In this parallel account of our stewardship passage, the unfaithful servant is not simply stripped of what little he has, but he is actually cast into outer darkness—what we can certainly conclude to be an image of Hell, where there is weeping and gnashing of teeth (great pain and anguish).

Let that serve as a warning. If you are an unfaithful steward, God is not interested in *why* you chose to disobey. If you're not tithing, "why" isn't going to help you when you stand before Him. If you're not faithfully giving offerings (Mal. 3:8), your reasons aren't going to vindicate you. It is **required**, not highly suggested or preferred, that a steward be found faithful.

The unfaithful steward is punished, plain and simple. So the matter is simplified to a series of choices that you need to make. Will you serve God or mammon (Lk. 16:13), because you can't serve them both? Will you let your financial issues manipulate you into being unfaithful over what doesn't belong to you in the first place, or will you persevere through temptation (Jas. 1:12) and arrive at the place called increase?

"Praise ye the LORD. Blessed is the man
that feareth the LORD, that delighteth
greatly in his commandments... [3]
Wealth and riches shall be in his house:
and his righteousness endureth forever."
Psalms 112:1-3

11

The Prosperity Mentality

We can talk about wealth all day long, but the reality is that if you want to walk in it—and consistently—it's going to require a change in your way of thinking. The Bible makes no mystery of the fact that our way of thinking is the primary front in the war of victorious living. In fact, the well-known "weapons of our warfare" passage in Second Corinthians 10:4-5 deals specifically with the war being waged in the mind.

If we plan on walking in financial prosperity, it's absolutely vital that we develop the mentality that goes along with it; otherwise, we'll be just like many lottery winners who win the jackpot one day and are dead broke a few years later (sometimes quicker).

I preached a message a few years ago entitled "Leaving Egypt". It dealt with the travesty of an entire generation of Hebrews being freed from Egyptian bondage only to wander in the wilderness for forty years because their way of thinking hadn't been freed along with their physical bodies. What good is a change of *status* without a change of *condition?*

Now, when I speak of developing the prosperity mentality, I'm not talking about simply reading this chapter and agreeing that everything I say is true. I'm talking about having a complete transfusion of your thought process, until the word of God literally becomes your personal viewpoint, your very way of thinking.

Whether it regards financial prosperity or any other subject, as a Christian, you should be committed to submitting your thinking to the word of God. It's one thing to want to do something wrong and yet do the right thing simply because it's the right thing to do. That ability comes with spiritual maturity. However, you've reached an entirely different level when you are so transformed in your thinking that you actually *want* what's right.

I'm tired of hearing people testify about a so-called blessing one day, and seeing them at the altar a few weeks later dealing with the spirit of lack. So, my goal in this chapter is to clearly explain why it's important that you don't simply do what's right when it comes to biblical prosperity, but that you cultivate the thought pattern that will firmly establish you in the wealthy place.

"Who Told You You Were Naked?"

I'm amazed that still today, many Christians don't realize that their way of thinking is directly connected to what they've been hearing. The Bible says that faith comes (or is developed) by hearing (Ro. 10:17). When you subject yourself to hearing certain things, after a while it transforms how you think.

228

This is why cults are so powerful. A cult doesn't program people by beating them in the head and forcing them to agree. It simply surrounds them with its teachings and restricts their ability to hear contrary points of view. When people are subjected to that level of indoctrination over long periods of time, they'll believe practically anything.

When I think about how important it is for Christians to take seriously what and who they allow to teach them, I can't help but think back to Adam and Eve. We all know the story—how Eve took of the forbidden fruit of the tree of the knowledge of good and evil and ate, and then gave it to Adam. Then, after their eyes were opened, they saw that they were naked and ashamedly hid themselves.

What's interesting about the story is what happened next. God called to them and Adam responded, telling God they were naked. Now, because Adam said they were naked, my first thought was that God would have replied, "Who *showed* you you were naked?" Since nakedness is a physical thing indicated by outward appearance, one would think that God's initial question would deal with the visual aspect of their nakedness. However, that wasn't the case.

> *"And they heard the voice of the LORD God walking in the garden in the cool of the day: and Adam and his wife hid themselves from the presence of the LORD God amongst the trees of the garden. [9] And the LORD God called unto Adam, and said unto him, Where art thou? [10] And he said, I heard thy voice in the garden, and I was afraid, because I was naked; and I hid myself. [11]*

And he said, Who told thee that thou wast naked? Hast thou eaten of the tree, whereof I commanded thee that thou shouldest not eat?"

Genesis 3:8-11

In the manner of God's question to Adam, I pose the following question to you: If you're not convinced that God wants you to prosper financially, who *told* you that? If the Bible didn't say it—and it definitely didn't—then somebody fed you that poison. Unfortunately, the primary perpetuators of such nonsense are not unbelievers. They're Christian teachers and preachers.

This has resulted in a tremendous problem in the body of Christ. You see, it's imperative that believers recognize the vital importance of the doctrine of financial prosperity. There's more hanging in the balance than most Christians realize.

Financial prosperity isn't simply about buying a new house or a new car. Does that play a part? Yes! Only someone who doesn't understand God's love would believe that He doesn't desire for us to have the best, especially when considering such passages as Psalm 84:11. It does not make God shallow or superficial to desire such things for us. But, although personal enjoyment of wealth plays a small part in financial prosperity, it is nowhere near the primary purpose of it. For that matter, it's not even the secondary purpose, as we discovered in Chapter 2.

The primary purpose of wealth is Kingdom expansion. So, if people around you are speaking *against* the prosperity message, especially if those people are in the pulpit of your local church, you need to re-evaluate your reasons for allowing those voices to continue to feed your spirit.

Both the prosperity message and the opposing *just enough* message have serious implications for the body of Christ. If you know of teachers and preachers who are pouring the poison of *just enough* into the minds of their listeners, you should purchase a copy of this book for them. If after allowing them an opportunity to be exposed to the truth on this vitally important subject, they persist in their beliefs, you'll know that their priorities are not where they should be.

The moral of the story… It is your responsibility to ensure that what you're subjecting your ears to is sound doctrine (Acts 17:11), especially when that doctrine is so important to the Kingdom. Surround yourself with people who speak the *whole* counsel of God, not just Calvary and Christian living.

Why Is The Right Mindset So Important?

The prosperity mentality is important for many reasons. First of all, you *must* understand that you aren't defined by the circumstances that surround you. One mistake we as Christians make is to define ourselves (or others) according to our present situations, never realizing that circumstances and situations are fleeting. Scripture reveals quite clearly that what actually defines us is our way of thinking.

We are the sum total of the thought processes we engage in. Proverbs 23:7 bears this out.

"For as he thinketh in his heart, so is he... Eat and drink,
saith he to thee; but his heart is not with thee."

Proverbs 23:7a

This passage relates how some people can speak friendlily to you, yet in their hearts, they don't care for you. How often have people said things to you that you knew were not a true representation of how they felt? Whether in romantic relationships, friendships, or even business associations, we've all experienced this to one degree or another. It's no wonder God isn't very concerned about what's expressed on the outside, but rather what's felt on the inside.

"But the LORD said unto Samuel, Look not on his
countenance, or on the height of his stature; because I have
refused him: for the LORD seeth not as man seeth; for man
looketh on the outward appearance, but the LORD looketh
on the heart."

1 Samuel 16:7

Child of God, it's not enough that you simply believe this prosperity teaching. Plenty of Christians *believe* that Jesus is Lord, but that doesn't imply that they live their lives as though it's really true. I challenge you to actually line up your thinking with this word to the extent that it becomes who you are as a person.

You can easily prosper in life at one point or another. God's purpose, however, is for you to prosper continually. But, the only way this will happen is for your way of thinking to be determined by His word.

> *"Beloved, I wish above all things that thou mayest prosper*
> *and be in health, even as thy soul prospereth."*
>
> *3 John 1:2*

Notice the principle involved in John's blessing—that our way of thinking (our soul) is directly related to the level of prosperity we can have in life. In other words, you will only prosper and be in health in proportion to the prosperity of your soul.

Now, your soul is your mind, your will, and your emotions. It is your way of thinking, your method of choosing, and your agency of feeling. So, what John was saying was that if your way of thinking is off, your finances and even your health can (and likely will) follow suit.

I've known many people whose physical health was directly affected by the state of their thought patterns. I've known bitter people to suffer bitterly (pun intended) in their health. I've also known happy, positive people who rarely had health issues. When you don't get your thinking in order (in harmony with God's word), it has a serious effect on everything else that concerns you.

Always remember this principle: Your way of thinking literally defines you as a person. So, the next time you bite your tongue but cuss someone in your mind, or the next time you smile and speak pleasantly to someone that you can't stand, remember that God's not impressed by the so-called level of discipline you think you're operating in (simply because you didn't verbally express your negativity). He's concerned with what's on the inside.

Just as a side note, Christians have become masters of the mask. We're professionals at smiling in people's faces and rolling our eyes on the inside. But, contrary to what we've been taught traditionally, not everybody deserves a smile. Just consider Jesus, who called the Pharisees hypocrites and a generation of vipers right to their faces. (Matt. 22:18; 23:23)

Back to the point at hand... If you don't develop the prosperity mentality, you will confine yourself to a life of mediocrity. Sure, there may be moments you experience abundance and excess, but they'll be temporary flukes. How often have you gotten a bonus at work, or received an unexpected check in the mail, only to see it gone with the wind?

"Wilt thou set thine eyes upon that which is not? for riches certainly make themselves wings; they fly away as an eagle toward heaven."

Proverbs 23:5

When you become a prosperity-thinker your wealth will be firmly established. Your testimony won't be "Here today... Gone tomorrow." You'll be able to say, "This is the Lord's doing, and it is marvelous in my eyes!"

Be Ye Transformed

You mustn't ever forget that the spiritual war is not being waged in the seen realm. It's being waged in your mind... in your way of thinking. You see, Satan knows that if he can control your thought process, he's got you.

> "For though we walk in the flesh, we do not war after the flesh: [4] (For the weapons of our warfare are not carnal, but mighty through God to the pulling down of strongholds;) [5] Casting down imaginations, and every high thing that exalteth itself against the knowledge of God, and bringing into captivity every thought to the obedience of Christ"
>
> 2 Corinthians 10:3-5

The purpose of the weapons of our warfare is to win the fight for our way of thinking. We're to cast down arguments and reasoning in our thinking that try to exalt themselves against what we know through Scripture to be right. We're to take our thoughts captive to the obedience of Christ, through His word. That's strong language, and it indicates the seriousness of the war we wage within.

I understand from experience how difficult it can be to change your way of thinking when God says something different than what you've thought all your life. In my case, a good example would be what qualifies someone to be a Christian. You see, I was raised under the teaching that being saved isn't a state of being, but a lifestyle. If one wasn't living the lifestyle, they weren't saved

Since those days, I've come to understand that being saved or not isn't determined by lifestyle. On the contrary, it has everything to do with the free gift given through the blood of Jesus. While being saved definitely *should* transform how we live our lives, we are neither qualified nor disqualified *because* of our lifestyle. Otherwise, we are no longer saved by faith, but rather, by works—a heretical doctrine, indeed. But, that teaching is another story altogether.

The point is that I understand how sometimes our immediate response to teachings that differ from what we've previously been taught is rejection, and oftentimes hostile rejection. But, I implore you… If you're resistant to the prosperity message, keep in mind that the messenger does not qualify the message. It's qualified solely by the word of God. Let His word be the sole determinate of what you will and will not accept, and don't hesitate to change your thinking when the word has spoken. That's when spiritual growth takes place.

"And be not conformed to this world: but be ye transformed by the renewing of your mind, that ye may prove what is that good, and acceptable, and perfect, will of God."

Romans 12:2

In the first verse of this chapter, the apostle Paul used the word "beseech" to describe the intensity with which he pled with the Roman believers. He understood that unless we allow our minds to be changed about some of the things we've traditionally thought, and unless we're transformed by God's word, we can't experience the good, acceptable, and **perfect** will of God in our lives. Now, to someone who loves God and wants to be pleasing to Him, this statement should prompt us to take action.

I want to take a moment and examine some of the thought patterns that characterize our old ways of thinking—things that must be changed if we're going to experience financial prosperity.

"Labor not to be rich: cease from thine own wisdom."

Proverbs 23:4

The world's way of obtaining wealth is to work long and hard for it. People have been known to literally work themselves to death trying to make as much money as possible. It's the world's way; and unfortunately, it's crept into the Church.

We, like the world, have allowed ourselves to be governed by the pursuit of wealth, and that is absolutely not God's way. So many Christians accept or reject job offers based primarily on how much the job pays. They overwork themselves with overtime because they want to buy a new car or that new HD television they've been eyeing for a few months (or to simply keep their debts paid to-date).

Many believers make important financial decisions without honestly consulting God for direction. What do they base their decisions on instead? You guessed it—money. As individuals and as a corporate body, the Church has become primarily money-driven, and that's a horrific admission.

Believers have defined their relationship with money according to the world's system. We claim to believe that debt isn't God's will for us, yet we willingly accept car notes, credit cards, and lines of credit as normal and necessary parts of life. It's no shock that the Body of Christ as a whole isn't walking in the wealth of God.

In this passage (Proverbs 23:4), God told us to "cease from [our] own wisdom." When it comes to wealth, He wasn't telling us to avoid riches, but rather not to work simply to *become* rich. That's the world's way of obtaining wealth, but not God's way.

The world's wisdom says that we should work to put food on the table, clothes on our back, a roof over our head, a car in our garage, and money in our pocket. God's wisdom, on the other hand, says that we should work to have more seed to sow, and to have more resources with which to build the Kingdom. As for food and clothes, He promised to take care of that if we would just have Kingdom priorities (Matt. 6:31-33). That may sound unwise, but the wisdom of God has always been foolishness to the carnal-minded. (1 Co. 2:14)

Something else we need to change in our traditional view of wealth is the notion that money is the enemy. For years, we have misquoted First Timothy 6:10 as saying, "…money is the root of all evil." That's not what the passage says at all, and this is a prime example of the importance of reading the word of God for yourself. What the passage says is that the *love* of money is the root of all evil. Money is neither good nor bad. It's your relationship with money that determines whether it serves a godly purpose.

Now, these were just two quick examples of common ways of thinking that have to be purged from our minds. Once we wash our old thought patterns with the water of the word (Eph. 5:26), we'll begin to see the will of God—as it relates to financial prosperity, as well as every other area—manifested in our lives.

Claiming The Blessing Of Abraham

"And I will make of thee a great nation, and I will bless
thee, and make thy name great; and thou shalt be a blessing:
[3] And I will bless them that bless thee, and curse him
that curseth thee: and in thee shall all families of the earth
be blessed."

Genesis 12:2-3

In this passage, God established a trans-generational promise to Abraham. This promise wasn't limited to him, and it wasn't limited to his children. It was and is an ongoing promise that continues to this very day.

What it's important we understand is the *application* of this promise. Most Christians can agree that this promise definitely applies to present day Jews, the natural descendents of Abraham. What some have not come to understand, however, is that through Christ, this promise jumped the natural bloodline and now covers all of the spiritual descendents of Abraham, as well.

While this sounds like good news, how does it affect us, the Church? Well, the Church itself is comprised of the spiritual descendents of Abraham. So, if you are a Christian (a born-again believer in Jesus), you are a recipient of this promise, a joint heir together with Christ Himself.

"Christ hath redeemed us from the curse of the law, being
made a curse for us: for it is written, Cursed is every one
that hangeth on a tree: [14] That the blessing of Abraham

239

might come on the Gentiles through Jesus Christ; that we
might receive the promise of the Spirit through faith... [29]
And if ye be Christ's, then are ye Abraham's seed, and
heirs according to the promise."

Galatians 3:13-14, 29

"And if children, then heirs; heirs of God, and joint-heirs
with Christ; if so be that we suffer with him, that we may be
also glorified together."

Romans 8:17

The previous passages clearly reveal that the very promise we read in Genesis 12 is extended toward us, the Body of Christ. Now, if the promise unto Abraham applies to us, all of a sudden we can read this passage with a whole new zeal. This isn't just God's promise to Abraham. If you're a believer, it's God's promise to YOU. Let's re-read this passage, and we're going to substitute our names in there to make it more personal.

"And I will make of Abraham a great nation, and I will
bless [YOUR NAME], and make [YOUR NAME]'s
name great; and [YOUR NAME] shalt be a blessing: [3]
And I will bless them that bless [YOUR NAME], and
curse him that curseth [YOUR NAME]: and in [YOUR
NAME] shall all families of the earth be blessed."

Genesis 12:2-3

First of all, God promised to make of Abraham a great

nation. We see that promise fulfilled in the nation that bore the name of his grandson both in Bible days and in present-day – Israel (Jacob's name after it was changed in Gen. 32:28). But, with our greater understanding of the application of this promise, we also see it fulfilled in the Church, who is also *of* Abraham.

In addition, God promised to *bless* Abraham. Not only would he be blessed, but he would *be* a blessing to others, even to all the families of the earth.

We examined the word "blessed" in Chapter 1; and in particular, how it applies to financial prosperity. If you recall, the *blessing* of the Lord makes the blessed person rich and doesn't add the sorrows that accompany riches obtained by people who don't have the blessing operating over their lives. But, now is a good time to further develop our understanding of the term.

The word "blessing" is a translation of the Hebrew word *berâkâh*, which simply means empowerment or enabling. This comes from the root *bârak*, which means "to empower to prosper".

A mistake many people make is that they look at wealth (or at the things that they acquire) and consider it the blessing. People often testify about how God "blessed" them with a new house, or a new job, or a spouse. But, these things are **not** blessings.

There's a big difference between the wind and the leaves blowing down the street as a *result* of the wind. In this analogy, the unseen wind is the blessing, not the result of the wind's presence— the blowing leaves. In the exact same way, the blessing is not the car or the house. It's not the healing you received, or the children you prayed to have. The blessing is the unseen supernatural

241

empowerment—what we call an *anointing* in Christianese—that enabled these things to come to pass in your life.

You need to clearly understand that your state of being blessed is not predicated upon—nor indicated by—your current situation. In the absence of a new car, you're *still* blessed. In the absence of a place to live, you're *still* blessed. The *empowerment* to prosper (the actual blessing) is upon you simply because you are a seed of Abraham and an heir of God.

But, how does this relate to the prosperity mentality? Well, it's very difficult to try to cultivate a mentality surrounding something you don't think you have a right to. It's important that you understand and apply the blessing of Abraham to your way of thinking.

When you claim the blessing of Abraham, it will change your perception of your finances. Knowing that you're *empowered* to prosper will change the way you make decisions, and the expectations you have for how things in your life will work out. You simply cannot do without understanding the blessing that's on your life, and applying it by faith over all you set your hands to accomplish.

Developing The Prosperity Mentality

Here are some practical steps you can take to develop the prosperity mentality in your soul.

Because faith comes by hearing the word of God (Ro. 10:17), it's vital that you saturate your environment with the word regarding prosperity. Buy audiotapes of teachings and play them through the day (e.g. on your way to work, while preparing dinner, etc.). The more you hear the word, the more your faith in the matter will be increased.

Something else I think is very helpful is taking notes when you listen to these sermons. But, that's not where it should end. Every few days (or at least every week), rewrite your notes. This will help you retain the information much quicker.

As you continue to study and commit yourself to this issue, make a conscious choice to agree with the word whenever it makes a point (whether it's what you've previously been taught or not). Then, make the decision to align your own way of thinking up with that word. Indeed, "be transformed by the renewing of your mind."

As you develop the prosperity mentality, you'll begin to see the effect it will have on your life. It can't help but transform your decision-making, your perceptions, even your relationship with God. It will stir up an appreciation and anticipation for what He's going to do in you, through you, and even *for* you. Before you know it, you'll begin walking in this thing, because as you think in your heart, so you are.

"This book of the law shall not depart out of thy mouth; but thou shalt meditate therein day and night, that thou mayest observe to do according to all that is written therein: for then thou shalt make thy way prosperous, and then thou shalt have good success."

Joshua 1:8

12

Cultivating The Giver In You

The many promises we have examined throughout the course of this book are made to the cheerful giver (with the exception of those that apply specifically to tithers). But, it's important to understand that there's a big difference between being someone who gives and actually being a giver.

You see, someone who gives simply engages in the act of giving from time to time. But, a giver is defined by his/her heart toward God and toward giving, not simply by acts of giving. Anyone can give from time to time, but not everyone has the heart of a giver. Not everyone is fulfilled when he gives.

It's a wonderful thing to give, whether you're a giver or not; but, God is really searching out givers—people He can trust to be faithful stewards and seed-distribution centers.

So, how do I become a giver? Unless you already know you're a giver, I hope this is the question you're asking right now. Hopefully, I've convinced you of the power of being a giver, both in pleasing

God (which is our primary aim), and in activating His promises over our finances. Because being a giver is a matter of the heart (rather than a matter of actions), you become a giver by cultivating the giver's heart.

A giver is one who doesn't need to be pumped and primed to give. His heart is already prepared to give, and he's quick to do so (1Ti. 6:18). In fact, a true giver seeks out opportunities to give, because this is his fervor, his passion. Finally, the giver recognizes that his giving is an act of worship, and he does it with consistency and cheerfulness.

I challenge you to become a giver. Cultivate the giver's heart, and make giving an act of worship. Be God's partner, a giver who is trustworthy, faithful, and an invaluable asset to the Kingdom.

The God-Kind of Giving

As we talk about giving, and the place it should have in our lives, the best example I can point out is God Himself. It seems rather unfair to hold ourselves to such a standard, but I'll tell you this—there is no better biblical example of a true giver than God.

First of all, we've spent considerable time examining just how liberally God gives to His believers. Not only does He give more and more seed to those He can trust to sow it, but He also gives those sowers bread for food. In Luke 6:38, He promised to give "good measure, pressed down, shaken together, and running over." His name, in fact, is El Shaddai, the God of All Provision. But, let's go even further and examine the type of giver God is.

When God created Adam, He gave of His own substance by breathing into him the breath of life (the *neshamah chay* – pronounced nesh-aw-maw´ kah´-ee), which literally translates as the living spirit. So, from the beginning, God was a giver, having given man something that nothing else in creation had—a spirit in His own image.

Then, God put Adam down in a garden prepared just for him. It's interesting to note that God made sure that wherever He put Adam, he would have everything he needed right there with him. He gave him fruit-bearing plants and trees for nourishment, four streams of water, and eventually, even a fitting companion.

Moving down through history, God miraculously gave manna from Heaven to the journeying Hebrews, even when they had been judged and forced to wander until an entire generation had passed away. Then, under the leadership of Joshua, God literally *gave* entire city-states to the Hebrews during their Canaanite conquest (e.g. Jericho).

So as not to spend too much time detailing the innumerable examples of God's giving, I'll jump ahead to the greatest gift He gave—Himself.

> *"For God so loved the world, that he gave his only begotten*
> *Son, that whosoever believeth in him should not perish, but*
> *have everlasting life."*
>
> *John 3:16*

We all know this very common passage, which shows us the

extent of God's love. In understanding the tri-unity of God, we know that He actually gave Himself as the sacrifice for our sins (1 Tim. 3:16), dying for people who wouldn't necessarily take advantage of His sacrifice. That's absolute love, and the heart of an absolute giver.

That's the kind of selfless giver God is calling for you to be. When you give, you should do so not in response to selfish desire, but out of a genuine love for God. If you're giving to ministry, it should be because you have a respect for the ministry you're giving to and have a sincere desire to help empower them in their service. You shouldn't give just so that you'll receive (although you can and should certainly have the joy and expectation of that promise). Your heart should be cheerful and your motives pure.

Exercising Faith In Your Giving

"For unto us was the gospel preached, as well as unto them: but the word preached did not profit them, not being mixed with faith in them that heard it."

Hebrews 4:2

This passage teaches a principle that you simply **must** understand. It's applicable to every area of life, not just to the issue of financial prosperity. The last thing you want to do is gloss over this section without fully digesting what's said.

Many Christians believe that going to church and hearing a message is all they need to do. But, Paul (the assumed author of this passage) said otherwise. He explained that what makes the word profitable in your life is not the act of hearing it, but the process of exercising faith in that word.

We see this very same principle borne out in the gospel account of Jesus returning to His hometown to minister.

> *"And when he was come into his own country, he taught*
> *them in their synagogue, insomuch that they were astonished,*
> *and said, Whence hath this man this wisdom, and these*
> *mighty works? [55] Is not this the carpenter's son? is not*
> *his mother called Mary? and his brethren, James, and Joses,*
> *and Simon, and Judas? [56] And his sisters, are they not*
> *all with us? Whence then hath this man all these things?*
> *[57] And they were offended in him. But Jesus said unto*
> *them, A prophet is not without honor, save in his own*
> *country, and in his own house. [58] And he did not many*
> *mighty works there because of their unbelief."*
>
> *Matthew 13:54-58*

Unfortunately, because of the people's personal familiarity with Jesus, He wasn't able to accomplish much ministry in their midst. It's sad commentary, indeed, when people let their familiarity with a minister of God keep them from receiving ministry from that individual.

I want you to notice something very important in this passage. What limited Jesus' ability to perform works was not His own belief, but the unbelief of the recipients of His ministry. He "did not many mighty works there because of ***their*** unbelief."

Yes, God's word is "quick, and powerful, and sharper than any two-edged sword," but if you don't mix that word with faith, it will not accomplish its intended purposes in your life. Apply this to the matter of financial prosperity as a whole, and in particular, to the issue of giving, and you'll see an important truth. If you don't exercise faith in your finances (and in your giving), you will not see the results God promised.

Giving is the highway to prosperity and faith is the vehicle by which you'll get there. The two go hand-in-hand. You can drive through the wilderness of aimless giving, or you can choose to take the path that God has already laid out. Exercise faith in your giving, and financial prosperity will be yours.

Now Faith Is...

It would be a great injustice for me to emphasize the importance of exercising faith in your giving, and then not tell you exactly how to do it. So first, I'm going to explain what faith is, and then show you how to apply it to your finances, and to your giving in particular (because that's the specific area Christians seem to have the most trouble with).

> *"Now faith is the substance of things hoped for, the evidence*
> *of things not seen."*
>
> *Hebrews 11:1*

Put simply, faith is an individual assurance and spiritual proof of a reality that has not yet manifested. Faith isn't simply believing God. Rather, it takes belief to the next level by allowing that belief to serve as proof that what is hoped for and unseen actually exists (has already been done). Faith puts belief to the test by making you respond as though what is hoped for actually has present substance, and as though what is not yet seen is already visibly manifested.

Belief says, "God will do it," whereas faith says, "God did it!" Belief awaits manifestation, whereas faith accepts it as a presently done deal and responds accordingly, even though physical proof doesn't exist. In fact, faith stands in as the **substance** (proof) of things hoped for, and it stands in as the **evidence** of things not yet seen. So, in the heart of a person of faith, there **is** proof that it's done, and that proof is the person's faith.

Belief looks forward to what God is going to do, whereas faith looks backward, believing it's already done and acting accordingly.

You may be thinking, *But, shouldn't belief be enough, considering that it's not like I don't trust that God will do it. Why must I move on it now, before I see it?* That's a valid question, and Scripture answers it fairly clearly in James 2:19, saying, "Thou believest that there is one God; thou doest well: the devils also believe, and tremble." In other words, God says to us, "Yes, you believe me, and that's good; but even the demons believe. My question to you is: Since you believe, what are you going to **do** about it."

You see, faith is all about taking present action on a belief, even though it hasn't manifested yet. Unlike mere belief, faith becomes all the manifestation you need to move forward. In fact, faith is not faith until it has produced corresponding actions. The Bible puts it this way: "Faith without works [corresponding actions] is dead." (Jas. 2:26) So, belief simply extends a trust that something will come to pass, but faith actually settles the issue in the heart of the believer and produces the corresponding actions (as though what is hoped for has already happened).

Faith isn't just an inward belief. You can **see** faith in the actions that it produces. In the absence of these corresponding actions, there is no real faith.

Faith In Action

In order for faith to produce physical manifestation, it must be put into action (exercised). You already know that "faith without works is dead," so now we need to look at the actual works that faith should be producing when it comes to your finances.

First of all, decisions must not be made according to your present condition. A sinner can do that. What makes a person of faith different is that they're able to create a different reality in their hearts and allow that believed reality to be what dictates their decisions rather than their present circumstance. **This is what faith is all about.**

So, when it comes to your giving, your offerings should **never** be dictated by the financial obligations you have. Now, keep in mind that I'm talking about offerings here. This does not include tithes or firstfruits, which we've already discovered aren't yours anyway, and should stand alone as monies in your possession that must be given back to the rightful owner—God.

Here's what most people do when it's payday. They sit down with their bills, add them up, and see what they can pay. The "faithful" Christians take their tithes off the top because they recognize that it doesn't belong to them, and then they pay their bills. Once they're done, they look at what's left and decide how much their offering should be. As we've seen in the first chapter of Malachi, however, this is **absolutely** the wrong approach.

Yes, tithes must come off the top, but so should the offerings. If God is not considered a higher priority than your mortgage, then you should pray to the mortgage company the next time you're sick. Remember that God isn't just robbed when we don't pay our tithes, but even when we withhold our offerings (or when we offer gifts of no substantial value to us—what Malachi calls the lame and deaf).

When it's time to decide how much to give in your offering, you should ask God. Whatever answer He returns, you should be quick to give it, no matter whether your financial state tells you it would be a foolish course of action or not.

"For the wisdom of this world is foolishness with God. For it is written, He taketh the wise in their own craftiness."
1 Corinthians 3:19

Now, there *will* be moments when God is silent regarding a specific amount to give. This does not mean that He doesn't want you to give. It simply means that He is leaving it to your own volition. These are opportunities to exercise faith with sacrificial offerings— amounts that demonstrate a willingness to see past the state of your finances and simply give as an expression of thanksgiving.

Just remember that if you don't give in faith, there will be no way to activate the blessings associated with God's promises concerning your finances. It's **impossible** to please God without faith, and since pleasing God is our utmost aim, it should be the driving force behind our acts of giving.

> ### An offering you feel comfortable
> ### giving is not an offering given in faith.

Most of what God will accomplish on your behalf will be as a result of your faith. In fact, even in the Gospels, Jesus did things for people not according to His will, but according to their faith. Jesus wanted to accomplish miracles in the midst of the Nazarenes, but He couldn't because of their unbelief. In addition, consider the following examples in which Jesus indicated the importance of the people's faith in order for them to receive a miracle:

> *"But Jesus turned him about, and when he saw her, he said,*
> *Daughter, be of good comfort; thy faith hath made thee*
> *whole. And the woman was made whole from that hour."*
>
> *Matthew 9:22*

"Jesus said unto him, If thou canst believe, all things are possible to him that believeth."

Mark 9:23

"And Jesus answered and said unto him, What wilt thou that I should do unto thee? The blind man said unto him, Lord, that I might receive my sight. [52] And Jesus said unto him, Go thy way; thy faith hath made thee whole. And immediately he received his sight, and followed Jesus in the way."

Mark 10:51-52

If you're not giving in a way that exercises faith, you're not tapping into the potential of what God wants to do in your finances. If you can learn to sow in tears—give amounts that stretch and challenge your faith—you can reap in joy. (Psalm 126:5-6)

"He that observeth the wind shall not sow; and he that regardeth the clouds shall not reap. [5] As thou knowest not what is the way of the spirit, nor how the bones do grow in the womb of her that is with child: even so thou knowest not the works of God who maketh all. [6] In the morning sow thy seed, and in the evening withhold not thine hand: for thou knowest not whether shall prosper, either this or that, or whether they both shall be alike good."

Ecclesiastes 11:4-6

I'll be the first to admit that giving is something you have to

255

grow into. It doesn't happen overnight. But, one of the biggest stumbling blocks people face when it comes to giving is that the primary determinate regarding the amount they give is not their heart towards God, but rather the other financial obligations they have. But, as we see in this passage in Ecclesiastes, this can be a stumbling block to the harvest.

When you're busy observing the wind and regarding the clouds—giving mind to your financial "climate"—you'll rarely so seed, and even then, it won't be much. Why? —Because until you develop the giving spirit, you'll likely always have bills to pay. When it comes to what you give to God, you need to raise your perceptions above the wind and clouds. Look only upon Him, and let your love for Him be what determines the amount you give, not the credit card company or even the mortgage.

Now, I'm not saying not to pay your bills. What I *am* saying, however, is that when it comes to giving, you cannot afford to let the amount be dictated by your other obligations. Remember, God's perfect will was for you to not have these other obligations in the first place, so far be it from you to allow them to usurp God's place as the first priority in your finances.

Also, as is borne out in verse 6, don't be afraid to give. So often, we fear giving because we're not sure if it's going to produce fruit in our lives. But, you never know how God may turn around your situation through a single act of obedience. While it's true that the harvest manifests after faithfulness and consistency, there are certainly times when He increases people after one particular act of giving. So, always be attentive to His voice, and always to "quick to give" (1Ti. 6:18 – rendered "ready to distribute" in the KJV).

Be Told...

Allow me to be pragmatic for a moment. It's easy for us "prosperity preachers" to tell you the ideal side of the message and leave out the negative (albeit temporal) implications. But, I would be doing you a disservice if I didn't tell you both sides.

I've seen too many people get angry with the prosperity preacher because although they did what the preacher told them to do, they didn't receive the promised harvest. I've seen people blame the preacher because they tithed when they could have paid their car note, and the car was repossessed, or they gave a sacrificial offering and wound up having to file for bankruptcy because lack persisted.

Let me preclude the possibility of you responding like many others if something negative happens after your acts of financial faith and obedience. First of all, God never once promised that bad things would never happen to good, faithful stewards. There are many times your faith will be tested because your enemy will try his hardest to get you to forfeit your harvest. He knows that only those who don't give up are promised the harvest. Don't let this scheme work!

Consistency is a requirement. You can't tithe 3 times and expect for your financial situation to turn around. Can it turn around in a short time? Absolutely. Will it happen in *your* case? Only God knows. Either way, you must continue to do what is right in God's eyes, not just because of the promise of a harvest, but simply because He's God, and what He says matters more than any negative thing that happens in your life in the meantime.

I myself have had a car repossessed when I could have paid the note if I withheld my tithe. I've had more utility cut-off notices than I'd care to discuss. I've had county sheriffs serve me with court papers because debt collectors were suing me. Yes, I've been there, and done that; and all of these things happened AFTER I became a faithful tither and giver.

But, I would never have begun receiving my harvest had I chose to exalt my financial situation above my God. I love Him, and I'm not going to allow **anything** to stop me from demonstrating that love through my financial faith and obedience.

If you tithe and give sacrificial offerings and still lose your house, there **is** a reason. Your loss could be the result of previous years that you didn't do the right thing with your finances. Don't forget that Paul stated that if we sow to the flesh, we will reap corruption (Gal. 6:8). So, a lack of results does not mean that God's word is not working. It could simply be that because "God is not mocked," you're still reaping corruption from previous periods of unfaithfulness.

Don't let such things stop you from doing what's right in God's eyes—primarily, just because it's right, and secondarily, because you're planting righteous seeds that **will** produce good fruit in due season (just as sure as the negative seeds eventually produced bad fruit).

Whatever you do, don't get upset with the preacher. He has absolutely zero power to make the promises of God come alive in your life. His job is to open your eyes to the truth. God has to take it from there.

258

The moral: I can't guarantee that nothing bad will take place after you start activating these principles. What I *can* guarantee, however, is that God is not a man that He should lie (Num. 23:19). If you keep doing what's right, you **will** reap a harvest when the time comes, *if you don't give up!*

*"And let us not be weary in well doing: for in **due** **season** we shall reap, **if we faint not**."*

Galatians 6:9 [emphasis mine]

"...May the Lord give ear to you in the day of trouble; may you be placed on high by the name of the God of Jacob; [2] May he send you help from the [sanctuary], and give you strength from Zion; [3] May he keep all your offerings in mind, and be pleased with the fat of your burned offerings; Selah. [4] May he give you your heart's desire, and put all your purposes into effect."

Psalms 20:1-4 (BBE)

Appendices

A

Practical Financial Wisdom

B

Common Questions Answered

C

Closing Remarks From The Pastor

A

Practical Financial Wisdom

After having completed this book, you may still be at a loss on where to begin. If reading through over 250 pages was a bit overwhelming, I understand. That's why I decided to add this appendix, the purpose of which is to provide you with practical steps you can take to start improving your financial situation.

Although money is not your source, it's still an important tool in your life. It's vital that you exercise financial wisdom so that bad decisions don't wind up counteracting the seeds you sow.

Wisdom and riches actually go hand-in-hand. Think about Solomon, who was the wisest man ever to have lived, and as a result of that wisdom also became the wealthiest man ever to have lived.

"The crown of the wise is their riches: but the foolishness of
fools is folly."

Proverbs 14:24

"With thy wisdom and with thine understanding thou hast
gotten thee riches, and hast gotten gold and silver into thy
treasures"

Ezekiel 28:4

"And by knowledge shall the chambers be filled with all precious and pleasant riches."

Proverbs 24:4

By educating yourself about financial matters from both a spiritual and practical perspective, you're positioning yourself for increase. Don't take this knowledge for granted. If you put it to wise use, I'll be smiling at your testimonial a year from now!

Here are some practical wisdom keys you can employ to help get you to the wealthy place. Just keep in mind that the principles discussed in the book cannot be summed up in the few points that will be included here.

DISCLAIMER: I am not a financial advisor. I have no formal financial training, so don't take my word here as "gospel". These are general suggestions on how you can get started in the process of improving your financial situation. I make or imply no guarantees.

Practical steps toward improving your finances:

1.   Budget... Budget... Budget

When many people hear the term "budget", they immediately think of some complicated, unrealistic approach to managing money. But, creating and maintaining a budget isn't as difficult as you may think, neither is it something you should do without.

If you don't know what's going out, and what's coming in, you'll never be in a position to make sound decisions, nor will you ever be able to handle the unexpected. Besides, I've seen by experience that when you see what you're spending money on in black and white, it'll probably shock you.

Most likely, there are many ways you can save. You just won't know it until you see what you're working with.

> *"Be thou diligent to know the state of thy flocks, and look well to thy herds."*
>
> *Proverbs 27:23*

For help with creating a budget, just log onto the Internet, visit www.google.com and do a search on "creating a budget" or "making a budget". This will pull up various sites that should be able to assist you with creating a budget. Now, if a particular site is not helping, don't be afraid to hit the back button (to return to your Google search results) and try a different website. You should definitely find the help you need.

Important Budgeting Tips

1) **Pay God First.** I know sometimes your finances may be dictating that you cannot afford to tithe (or pay your firstfruits), but you need to remember a few things. First, it's not an option for the God-loving believer. Honor

Him by ensuring that He's always the first priority. Second, your act of tithing is only the beginning on activating the promises of God concerning your finances. Don't give up before you've even begun.

2) **Give To God Second.** After you've paid God (the tithe and firstfruits), you now need to decide how much to *give* Him. Remember: Your gifts to God should not be an indication of how many bills you have. It should simply be an expression of your gratitude toward Him. Don't let the fact that you're in debt limit your giving, because that would be the equivalent of making your debts a higher priority.

3) **Pay Yourself Third.** That's right. Before anyone else should be paid, you should. Commit to an affordable monthly amount to put away for emergency purposes. This amount may be only $20/mo, but it's important that you maintain some type of emergency fund. If you get paid twice per month and can put away $20 or so per paycheck, that would be even better.

What's the value of an emergency fund? Unexpected things happen. That's life. You don't want to make the horrible mistake of using a credit card or getting a payday loan to deal with those occurrences. Having money put away is a great help.

Some people believe your emergency fund should be between $200-500 dollars. I personally believe you should keep giving to it indefinitely. Maybe after $500 have accumulated, you can start paying yourself by investing the $20-40/mo into an investment account (e.g. brokerage, mutual fund, or retirement account).

If you absolutely cannot afford to pay yourself because of the level of debt you're in, then I'd suggest skipping this step until your next income tax refund. Then, seed your emergency fund with the total amount you'd like to have put away (preferably around $500). –Yes, that means you won't be able to do all those things with your income tax refund that you wanted to do; but hey, if you don't mind being in debt the rest of your life, do what you want… Just remember that such an attitude is a poverty inducer.

4) **Pay Your Bills Fourth.** I know you may want to have money for recreational purposes, but you need to get out of debt first. *Maybe* you can allocate $20 or so **per month** for recreation, but aside from that, you really need to focus on being freed from financial bondage.

Don't forget that gasoline (if you drive a car), food, and personal hygiene are necessities, as well. They should all be included in your bill allotments.

267

5) **Cut Unnecessary Spending.** This is a difficult, but absolutely necessary step. The key in creating a budget is to see your spending in black and white. Once you're able to see where your money is going, do your best to cut away (or at least minimize) any non-essential spending.

Example Cutbacks:
- Gas (stay home or carpool when you can)
- Sell your SUV and get a smaller car
- Cut off your telephone features
- Dump the cellular or go prepaid for emergencies only
- Downgrade your cable or satellite plan
- Take your lunch to work
- Kill your pet (just kidding)
- Stop eating out (maybe once per month or per quarter)
- In the summer, turn the thermostat to 80° when away
- In the winter, turn the thermostat to 60° when away

6) **Get A Second Job If Necessary.** If, after cutting spending, you still don't have enough income to meet your monthly obligations, you'll need to find another source of income (usually, a second job).

A second job could be as simple as landscaping, building a small online business, or anything else you can think of. Traditional employment is always best because you can have a steady, dependable secondary income, which you can use to pay off enough bills to pull your budget into the black. This means that the entire paycheck (minus your tithes, firstfruits, and offerings) must be put toward paying down your debts.

Now, if you can keep the second job long enough to totally pay off all your lines of credit (credit cards, personal loans, car notes, and possibly even the mortgage) that would be great. At the very least, keep it long enough to pay off the smaller balances, like the credit cards and car loan.

2. Don't Be Afraid To Invest (Live For Tomorrow)

I'm not a financial advisor, but I can tell you that *relatively* safe investing is a great way to improve your finances. You may consider investing in a mutual fund. I don't have much more to add to this point, but I don't want to minimize its importance, either. Contact a financial advisor for assistance.

And no, investing is not the same as gambling. The latter is the result of get-rich-quick motivations, which the Bible clearly condemns (Prov. 28:20). The former speaks of sound, long-term financial strategy (in which you're actually part owner of a company, in the case of owning stock). Investing is not condemned in the Scriptures.

3.   Diversify

Don't put all your eggs in one basket. What if the basket breaks? When your regular fulltime job is your only source of steady income, you're walking on dangerous ground. You should have multiple streams of income. For example, one person could have money coming in from stock investments, a small Internet business maintained in spare time, real estate investments, and from a traditional fulltime job.

Find out ways to increase your streams of income. If one well runs dry, you'll still have others to drink from (at least until you get the other flowing again).

> *"Give a portion to seven, and also to*
> *eight; for thou knowest not what evil*
> *shall be upon the earth."*
>
> *Ecclesiastes 11:2*

4.   Be Content With What You Have

The single-greatest inducer of debt is greed. In Western culture, we've been programmed to value life by the quantity and quality of things we have. We must deprogram ourselves.

Learn to simply be content with what God has already given you. More will come in due time, but make it your priority to get out of debt first.

> *"Not that I speak in respect of want: for I have learned, in*
> *whatsoever state I am, therewith to be content. [12] I know*
> *both how to be abased, and I know how to abound: every*
> *where and in all things I am instructed both to be full and to*
> *be hungry, both to abound and to suffer need."*
>
> *Philippians 4:11-12*

5. Don't Cosign A Loan

When it comes to money, the only person you can depend on is yourself (and God, of course). Don't risk your own efforts to pull yourself out of the financial muck by cosigning a loan for someone else, even if it's your own child. The only exception would be if you have the money sitting around so that in the event the person doesn't pay, you can pay the loan yourself without a problem. But, in such an event, I'd wonder why you wouldn't just provide the money yourself and make the person pay you back rather than risking your credit rating. (Be sure to sign a contractual agreement if you go this route.)

> *"Be not thou one of them that strike hands, or of them that*
> *are sureties for debts. [27] If thou hast nothing to pay, why*
> *should he take away thy bed from under thee?"*
>
> *Proverbs 22:26-27*

6. Pay Your Bills

It is immoral to accumulate debt and not pay it. Not only did the Paul tell us in Ro. 13:8 to owe no man, but in the previous verse, he told us to "pay everyone what you owe them." People don't like to deal with this aspect of the prosperity message, but one part of being a good steward is having integrity, and not paying people their money isn't the best demonstration that.

I know from experience how frustrating collection calls can be. But, don't forget that they're calling because you owe them. Most collectors will work with you if you need a payment plan, so stop avoiding their calls. Stop paying extra money for caller ID just so you can avoid paying others their money.

7. Stop Borrowing Money

One thing Christians really need to stop doing is borrowing money. How can you get *out* of debt when you keep incurring it? Is God totally against borrowing of any kind? No. But, borrow only in the case of absolute need, not in the case of "kinda need" or "really really want".

A debt mentality will never produce increase in your life. Although you may come to possess more "things" through debt in the here and now, the spirit of bondage that comes along with those things will make them not worth the trouble.

Adopt the following mantra:

> *If God didn't give me the money to buy it,*
> *the property or skills to trade for it,*
> *or the favor to get it for free,*
> *He must not want me to have it*
> *—at least not right now.*

8.   Remember The Principles Governing Prosperity

Don't forget all the valuable spiritual principles we discussed
in this book. It's easy to get to this section and not look back,
but without activating the prosperity principles so that they
can undergird your efforts, none of this other stuff will matter
much. Keep in mind that the world's wisdom is not to be
valued above God's, for He uses the foolish things of the
world to make the world's wisdom look stupid. (1Co. 1:27)

B

Common Questions Answered

Q: ***Is it a sin to be in debt? Are there any types of
debt that are okay?***

A: The quick answer is: No, it's not; but ***please*** do not stop
reading here. Try not to think about this issue in terms of sin
and not sin; rather, think about it as right or wrong. Any and
all types of financial debt are outside of God's perfect will
(Ro. 13:8). We know for a fact that the borrower is servant to
the lender (Prov. 22:7), so there's no way to legitimatize
borrowing as a perfectly acceptable practice for God's people
(Matt. 6:24).

As I stated in Chapter 6, mortgage loans are different in that
they allow you to build equity (value in a home that exceeds
the amount due). It's only wise to spend $700/month
building equity in a home you own, rather than renting a
home at the same rate, and owning nothing.

Q: ***Should I only give to tax-deductible ministries?***

A: No. Never once in the Scriptures is even the faintest hint
given that you should only give to ministries that the
government has determined worthy of exemption. In fact, in

order to qualify for exemption, ministries have to agree to certain functional limitations. I have seen how the government uses tax exemption as a means to indirectly (and sometimes directly) manipulate ministries. So, if a ministry is not tax deductible, who cares (rhetorically)? If God put it on your heart to contribute, do so. The few bucks you'd be able to receive in your tax return through a deduction isn't worthy to be compared to the blessing that giving will produce in your life. Don't let government classifications or the lure of personal gain (tax deductions) stop you from contributing to ministries you wish to help.

Q: ***Do I have a right to see the financial statements of ministries I sow seeds into?***

A: No, you do not. Many people will take issue with this answer, but it's a biblical reality nonetheless. Although secular institutions believe that tax-exempt organizations answer to "the people", the Bible makes it clear that ministries only answer to God. If a ministry has been a blessing in your life through teaching, counseling, or in some other way, why should you have to see its financial statements in order to plant a seed? If a ministry is not a faithful steward over the funds received, God will deal with it (and He'll deal more harshly than anyone else ever could). You just activate the principles of giving, and let God take care of the rest. Those Christians who dedicate their lives to "exposing" the supposed financial indiscretions of Christian ministries do not have a mandate from God to do so, especially when they publicly attack these ministries (1Co. 6:1-8).

Q: ***Should I tithe off of my gross or net pay?***

A: You should tithe off of your gross pay (before-tax). Otherwise, you would be honoring the government above God. Also, if you tithe off of your gross pay, you will not need to tithe off of your income tax refund (if applicable) because the funds refunded have already been tithed.

Some people choose to tithe off of their net pay for more immediate access to funds, and then tithe off of their income tax check, but that still is not biblical for a few reasons. First, the tithe should be the first consideration of our funds. We must not delay a portion of the tithe until the annual tax refund. Second, the government only refunds the tax *over*payment. This says nothing about the portion of your taxes that the government actually keeps, nor any other payments taken out of your paycheck (e.g. retirement plan, medical insurance, etc.). So, by tithing off of your net and off of your refund check, there's still a portion not tithed at all.

Q: ***I own my own business. Should I pay tithes off of my business earnings, as well?***

A: This is not an uncomplicated answer, so I will try to make it as clear as possible. The short answer is: Yes. However, *how* you pay business tithes also needs to be addressed. Most people believe that you should only pay tithes on your profits, not on your business' entire income. Personally, I choose to tithe *all* my business' income because I feel that God provided the income, so I need to honor Him with it. Besides, the same argument could be used to justify paying tithes on personal income after deducting essential living expenses (housing, utilities, food), which would obviously be wrong.

Now, you probably also want to know if you should tithe your personal *and* business income. The answer depends on the legal structure of the business you operate. If you operate a sole proprietorship, the money is all yours, so it only needs to be tithed once (as personal income). If you operate a corporation, the business legally exists as a separate entity, so it should tithe off of its income, and you should tithe off of yours.

Now, at first glance, this may seem as though you're being made to tithe off of the same money twice. But, you're not. You have to remember that corporate funds are totally separate from personal funds. So, by tithing the business' income, you are acknowledging God as the source of income for the business entity. By tithing the personal pay, you are doing the very same thing you'd do by tithing pay received from *any* company you'd work for.

Q: *If I stop tithing during a rough financial period,*

do I have to pick up where I left off and catch myself up, or can I start fresh again?

A: This question is best answered by James 4:17. If you were not tithing because you did not know that the tithe belonged to God, He does not impute that as sin against you. But, once you know that God requires the tithe, you are responsible to pay it consistently. If you miss any tithes, God considers you a thief (Mal. 3:8-9). You can be forgiven, but you must still make restitution.

So yes, if after coming to the knowledge of the truth regarding tithing, you cease to tithe, you must "play catch-up", because until such time as you are caught up, your debt to God remains outstanding.

Q: ***Does God really charge me a 20% penalty if I miss a tithe?***

A: It is true that under the Law, a 20% penalty was assessed for a missed tithe (Lev. 27:13). However, this penalty is not applicable to the Christian Church. During Old Testament times, people tithed out of obligation to the Law, and just as with secular law, breaking the Law of Moses carried penalties. But, Christians have no business tithing (or giving in general) out of obligation. Our driving force should be love. Therefore, for the Christian, the penalty of refusing to tithe is equivalent to the refusal to obey any of the other requirements God has of believers. (Gal. 6:8)

Q: *Are Christians who do not tithe "cursed with a curse" as Hebrews were under the Old Covenant?*

B: This is certainly a good question, but I must say that before answering it, I feel compelled to point out that you should not tithe out of fear of being cursed. You should tithe out of a true and genuine love for God, a love that is best expressed not through a spirit of fear, but through a heart of obedience. That having been said, the reality is that being under the New Covenant does not exempt Christians from being cursed. When the Bible says that Christ took away the curse of the Law, it was talking about the overall curse that the Law, by its very nature, wrought over the people. It was also dealing specifically with people who were doing things out of *obedience* to the Law, rather than out of an understanding of the New Covenant (Gal. 3:10). We tithe not out of obedience to the Law, but out of our love for God, and our recognition of Christ's continuing priesthood.

For those who say that if we *do* tithe, we are cursed according to Gal. 3:10, I respond that they are not being consistent in their interpretation. Not fornicating was also commanded under the Law, but we certainly are not to fornicate even under the New Covenant, too. We don't maintain sexual purity out of obedience to the Law, but out of our love for God. In the same way, just because we continue to tithe does not mean that we are doing so out of obedience to the Law. Rather, our love for God and our recognition of Christ's continuing priesthood should compel us.

Now, with regard to the curse of Mal. 3:9, and whether Christians who do not tithe are cursed, consider that it's not until Rev. 22:3, when we have entered into eternity, that there will be no more curse. This indicates that even through the Church Age, people can have a supernatural empowerment to fail (a curse) operating in their lives, rather than a supernatural empowerment to succeed (a blessing).

When Malachi 3:9 said that those who do not tithe are cursed with a curse, it included a qualifying statement. According to the passage, the curse is a result of robbing God. As New Testament Christians who do not tithe are robbing God, it would seem that they also are brought under this same curse.

Fortunately, we have a great High Priest who pleads our case before the throne when we sin, begging divine mercy. But, it doesn't change the fact that robbing God still carries consequences, as does all sin. We must remember that God is *not* mocked. That which a man sows, he shall reap. If he sows to the flesh in disobedience to God's word, he will reap corruption, plain and simple (Gal. 6:7-8).

C

Closing Remarks From The Pastor

From The Desk of: Pastor R. D. Weekly

Date: February 5, 2008

Greetings in the name of the Lord Jesus, the source of all light, all hope, and all increase.

I would like to take this opportunity to challenge you to get the full benefit from what you've just read. The promises of God will not produce fruit in your life just by virtue of the fact that God made them. If such were the case, there would be no need for spiritual laws to exist—laws that require you to plant a seed in order to reap a harvest. You must put what you've learned into consistent action if you want God's promises to manifest in your life.

I strongly recommend that you re-read this book from time to time so that you can keep these principles at the forefront of your mind and heart. A wealth of information has been covered, so invest the time necessary to ensure that you glean all you can.

Never forget that the harvest is only guaranteed to those who make seed-sowing a habit. Except in the rare cases that God gives a substantial return after a single seed sown, faithfulness and consistency must be proven over time. Galatians 6:9 testifies that those who reap the harvest are those who "faint not". If you want to see results, you've got to keep on giving. That's why it's important to have a giver's heart, because if all you're after is a return, you've reduced God's economic system to a stock market.

On a personal note, I wish to thank you for purchasing this book. I also ask that you tell your family and friends about this resource so that God's word on finances can get out to the Body of Christ. It's in **knowing** the truth that we are made free, so help others know the truth regarding their finances by letting them know about this book.

In addition, please take a moment and visit the following website for more information about my ministry.

www.judahfirst.org

Finally, I can't fully express how encouraging it is to hear from you. If you've been blessed by what you've read, please contact me and let me know. You can do so through my ministry's website.

May God's blessings overtake you as you consistently apply these principles in your life.

Yours in the love of Christ,
Pastor R. D. Weekly